Revised – December, 2009

This printing – October, 2016

Direct all comments or suggestions to:

Royal Mountain Ministry

606 Bonita Way   •   Prescott, AZ 86301

www.RoyalMountainMinistry.com

RMM@RoyalMountainMinistry.com

How lovely on the mountains are the feet of him who brings good news, who announces peace and brings good news of happiness, who announces salvation, and says to Zion, "Your God reigns!"

Isaiah 52:7

CONTENTS

INTRODUCTION

T here is a common factor to most of   life's conflicts and the good news is that there is a simple solution. Please notice, I said simple, not easy. Though the answer is so uncomplicated a child can make it work, it will take determination and persistence to form this truth into new habits.

God designed human beings with:

1. Needs

2. Abilities

3. Authority

4. Responsibilities

These four areas will overlap through out our life and provide us with oppor-tunities for growth. Life is a test, a huge classroom of situations that teach, refine, and reveal   our inner character.   We were created by God to give Him pleasure and as we draw from His provisions for each test, He is pleased. This process of drawing from His resources is called faith:

And without faith it is impossible to please Him, for he who comes to God must believe that He is and that He is a rewarder of those who seek Him. Hebrews 11:6

So let us come boldly to the throne of our gracious God. There we will receive his mercy, and we will find grace to help us when we need it. Hebrews 4:16 nlt

As I see the inter-workings of the four areas of our design, I believe that God has placed some needs in us that are beyond our ability to meet and thus a choice is put before us. In the Garden of Eden this choice was between the fruit of two trees:

Knowledge..**Life**

Man was to reach for life, which would require continual dependence upon God. However, Adam and Eve were given the opportunity to try knowledge which would offer the appearance of independence, but the end result of true knowledge would be the reality that without the Lord we can do nothing (John 6:63).

In this classroom of life, our "needs" are to continually prod us

into the Father's waiting grace. His grace is sufficient for every need we will ever have (compare Hebrews 4:16 with 2 Corinthians 12:9). The Apostle Paul shared this truth with a bunch of idol worshipers one day in Athens, Greece:

The God who made the world and everything in it is the Lord of heaven and earth and does not live in temples built by hands. {25} And He is not served by human hands, as if He needed anything, because He Himself gives all men life and breath and everything else. {26} From one man He made every nation of men, that they should inhabit the whole earth; and He determined the times set for them and the exact places where they should live. {27} God did this so that men would seek Him and perhaps reach out for Him and find Him, though He is not far from each one of us. {28} For in Him we live and move and have our being. As some of your own poets have said, "We are His offspring."

Acts 17:24-28 niv

Life is all about our choices. What will we reach for to meet our needs? Lessons have tests to see how well we learn the lesson, and in life, our main tester is our adversary, the devil. Through out this material I will continually warn you not to get sidetracked with the tester, but to quickly make the right choice, which includes dismissing the tester.

There is a dynamic link between responsibility and authority. In fairness, we can only be held accountable for that which we have the power to do something about. We've been given more authority over our environment than we have any idea. In fact, it's taken many thousands of years for us to discover that we can fly, alter DNA, and invent limitless products from the raw materials God has provided. And our authority also extends into the unseen world of the spirit!

Adam and Eve got into massive trouble when they failed to understand and use the authority each of us has been given over the tester. They could have chased him out of the garden instead of listening to his lies. But more on that later. This book is all about the authority that everyone has been given at birth and that is intensified as we enter into the special relationship with God called salvation.

When we reach for the wrong solutions to meet our needs or fail to use our basic authority to resist the tester and his assistants, we get into trouble – sin. When we follow the principles outlined in the Bible, we experience abundant life. It's really quite simple – simple, but not always easy.

When we see that there is something we can do about the pressures of life, when it finally gets through to us that the fastest way to pass a test is to reach out for our loving God, then life switches from survival to enjoyment. God has a Tree of Life near us at all times – we'll learn how to reach for His answers first. This needs to be a habit; a way of life.   It is supposed to be much easier to win the inner war than what most of us experience. I call the struggles of life the Inner War, because the battle is almost entirely won or lost in our thinking. There was a tremendous battle that Jesus fought for us on the cross; now the battle is in our minds to possess and enjoy what He paid for.

There are major differences between what the Bible says about the causes and cures for man's problems compared with secular psychology. The world has almost always gone opposite of what the Word teaches, from the Garden of Eden right up to today. Let me give you a few examples.

THE WORLD SAYS	THE WORD SAYS
Man is basically good	Men are born sinners
There is no God	God is all powerful
Survive at all costs	Put God first at all costs
We're our own worst enemy	Satan is our worst enemy
It's no fun being a Christian	Happiness is serving Jesus
Others give us inner wounds	Our responses can hinder inner healing
Talk out your problems	Cast your burdens on the Lord

Talking about the past helps   Jesus heals the past

There is nothing after death   There is a final judgment

Do you disagree with any of these comparisons?

Which of these do you feel causes the most problems for people? Why?

Can you think of any more contrasts between the world and the Bible?

THE PRESSURE OF PERSPECTIVES

Part of the inner war is the conflict between how we see life and how we think it should be. We have an idea in our minds of the ideal, how things **should** be. Our perspective of how things ought to be can pressure us to manipulate, correct, challenge, or fight others. We can expend much energy by trying to make the world around us into what we think it should be. How a person sees their home environment will put pressure on them to make others change, or at the very minimum, seek to persuade them to agree with their point of view. If they are vocal, they'll probably nag others. If they are the quiet type, they will play sneaky games. If they feel overwhelmed by the challenge, they'll collapse into despair, depression or sickness.

Think about what irritates you the most with the people closest to you. Could there be a perspective difference?   What?

Is someone always trying to get you to "see things" their way? Give an example:

Can you think of any of your perspectives that may be causing you unnecessary inner conflict?

How easy would it be for an enemy to make us angry or miserable? All they would have to do would be to make us think things were worse than they really are. Exaggerations and extremes are thoughts that cause many a brain cramp.

The Bible describes an aggressive, evil foe who sneaks around sticking pain-causing thoughts in our heads. Yes, there is a devil and he and his assistants are very busy. In the chapters ahead we'll look more into how the enemy works and how to shut him down. For now, consider how he and his crew can increase our inner pain by tempting us with unrealistic expectations or by painting negative, hopeless pictures.

SELF-TALK

Our mind mulls over, ponders and examines information all the time. We think about what we are seeing, feeling, and hearing. We may contemplate old pains from the past with a view to understanding what caused the pain, how could things have been done differently, "Why did this have to happen to me?", etc. This is not bad, in fact it one of the ways we grow and mature. But, think of the great damage that can be done by merely putting into someone's mind lies or half truths as they are going through this reflecting process. All our enemy has to do to produce great mental anguish is to distort our thinking. I call his input **stinkin' thinkin'**.

Emotional freedom will result as we learn:

- where negative input comes from
- how to compare our thoughts with God's Word

- how to eliminate destructive thoughts
- how to consistently ponder positive, godly thoughts.

Hurts from the past can be greatly amplified by a nagging spirit that tries to drive us crazy with <u>replays</u> and <u>reruns</u>. If we don't consider the enemy as a factor in our thought life, we'll be tempted to say that our self-talk seems to dwell on past hurts, turning over every rock to see why people did what they did and how we might have responded differently. Often the inner chatter is like a recording, playing hurtful, embarrassing memories over and over. It is my understanding of the Bible that when we do not want such brain-pain, the source of the irritation is more than likely from an ancient foe — the devil!

If this is so, then little will be gained by paying attention to him rehashing our embarrassing memories, and much relief will be quickly enjoyed by chasing him off.

The typical response to negative thoughts is to take the blame for them. The question I would ask is, "If you don't like the memories, and you don't enjoy pain, then why are you bringing them up?" If you don't like them, then maybe it's not you. Who could it be? Do we have an opponent? Is the same enemy tempting us that tempted Jesus? Is something going on behind the scenes in the invisible, spirit world?

WARNING:

Fighting is wearisome work, be it physical or spiritual. This is why we are told to Submit to God before we're instructed to resist the devil (James 4:7). To draw near to God (James 4:8) renews our strength (Isaiah 40:29-31). Please be careful not to give the enemy much time or credit. We will be explaining his workings so that you can more efficiently fight the foe, but you must not spend time focusing on him—rather, be taken up with your loving Heavenly Father.

If you start to feel drained or defeated because of spiritual warfare, or if you catch   yourself becoming "devil-minded," stop and realign your focus

— Hebrews 12:2—Jesus. See Isaiah 26:3.

Chapter 1

THE MAIN SOURCE OF HARASSMENT

Once upon a time there was a mad scientist named Serpetus. He was brilliant, powerful, but very cruel. He wanted to be in control of everything and everybody. Serpetus took great delight in sabotaging people's lives. He arranged for them to have auto accidents by tampering with their cars at night. He would access banks' computers and alter people's account balances, thus causing much turmoil. He even put diabolical viruses in the city's water supply and caused thousands to get very sick.

The one nemesis of Serpetus was that he couldn't get the people to stay sad. Somehow, after each tragedy, they would band together, encourage each other, sing a bit, dance around, and go on their way as though nothing of any significance had happened. This infuriated Serpetus. When they turned his evil into an occasion for joy, he was livid. His sinister mind was bent on hurting people, and he continually pondered new, diabolical ideas.

One day it came to him. "Ah yes, I will invent a small receiving device, so microscopic that it will be undetectable, and I will plant it in people's ears. Then I will whisper all sorts of crazy thoughts to them and drive them mad." He was absolutely thrilled with his new project and worked around the clock inventing a microscopic micro-chip that would act like a imperceivable radio to deliver his devilish input to each citizen in the city.

Because he was such a brilliant and powerful scientist, the task was soon finished and it was an easy matter to install the devices in each person's inner ear. He would put a special sleeping gas in their air conditioner and when they were unable to awake, would enter their house, install the devices, and then be on his way. He was having a ball.

The once happy city soon had a different atmosphere. People were suddenly rude, hateful, stingy, and always fighting. Serpetus would spy on a family and begin to make suggestions to the different family members via his implants.

One couple, newlyweds, were so much in love, and they, in particular, drove Serpetus crazy. He took them on as a unique challenge. Could he get them to hate each other? Could he break them up?

Willy and Barb were so much in love that they would sometimes sit and just look at each other. They enjoyed the same things. They went out of their way to make the other one happy — the ideal couple. But, thanks to Serpetus, things started changing. Willy began to notice things that Barb did, that irritated him. He knew she was not always the neatest housewife, but now, that seemed to be a big deal. He caught himself thinking, "What a slob; she never cleans anymore." Things were just like always, but now it seemed to matter to Willy.

Something strange happened when he shared this new insight with Barb. She seemed hurt. Inside her head, the simple "insight" Willy shared, was as big as an atomic bomb. She found herself thinking, "What's going on here? Have I been fooled all along that Willy really loved me for who I was? Maybe Marge was right when she told me our relationship could never last like this."

When Willy came home from work the next night, he was shocked to see the house more of a mess than it ever had been. No supper aroma filled the air. Barb sat curled up in front of the TV watching a panel of racists being interviewed by a show host. She glanced up and said, in a very detached manner, "Hi hon. I was tired and thought that maybe we could go out and get something to eat."

Why was this so different? Willy was so angry inside. He heard himself saying things to Barb that he didn't really believe. Where did the anger come from? Where did the feelings come from? What had changed their "ideal" relationship? Soon, Barb was crying and threatening to leave and go to her mom's.

*   *   *   *

If someone could put thoughts into people's minds, what kinds of trouble could they cause? For Willy and Barb, their marriage took a rapid turn for the worse. Have you seen a couple like Willy and Barb who fell in love with each other, in spite of each other's flaws, and then later grew to despise the problems they once overlooked? If so, what kind of thoughts do you think produced the friction in the relationship?

WELCOME TO THE REAL WORLD

We have a very angry enemy and his pleasure comes from destroying people. What he can't do by attacking our health, finances, etc., he has been able to do quite easily by whispering things to us. No, he doesn't use micro-chip implants; he uses his demons. The fallen angels, because they are spirits, can pass through us, virtually unnoticed, and whisper all sorts of weird things. If we are ignorant of how they work, we will more than likely receive their input as though it was our own "original" thoughts.

Even if the negative thoughts that "pop up" in our mind are of our own origin, when we ponder them, poison is released in our whole system. The Bible puts it this way:

For the mind set on the flesh is death, but the mind set on the Spirit is life and peace.

Romans 8:6 nas

When devilish "insight" is contemplated in our mind, stinkin' thinkin' will be   the outcome. *This is how many of our perspectives are formed.* And, along with perspectives come feelings. This verse is clearly telling us that death results when our mind focuses on the flesh (which is a metaphor for stinkin' thinkin'). This "death" can kill marriages, friendships, and even compromise one's immune system, thus endangering their health. Have you ever sensed the enemy's input? I mean, have you caught a thought that popped into your head and it was something you did not want?

AN OVERVIEW

There are four very important things we must understand if we are going to win this inner war:

1. **We have an aggressive enemy** that whispers all sorts of things to us. His lies can **only** hurt us when we believe them and act accordingly.

2. If we're a Christian, we're a new person in Christ. We no longer want to do hurtful, wicked things; therefore, **when gross thoughts pops into our head, it most likely is from the enemy.**

3. Something must be done, not only with the harmful thoughts that pop into our head, but also with the messenger that delivers them. Serpetus' implants must be removed. **I must resist the thoughts and bind the messenger!**

4. **New thinking patterns must replace old ones.** Selfish, self-protective thoughts must be replaced with prayer, praise and pondering the life-giving promises of God's Word.

Later we'll examine in more detail the second point, that if we are a Christian, we really do not want the hurtful thoughts that suddenly appears in our mind. But, let me just say now that not all of the negative thoughts that appear in your mind are your doing. Some are, of course, but not as many as you may think. If you have been hard on yourself because you thought you were your own worst enemy, please declare a "cease fire" until I can present my evidence. Then if you don't agree with me, go back to your rough treatment of yourself. Or, in terms of the example with Willy and Barb, don't assume the honeymoon is over until you hear me out. Fair enough?

I don't presume that everyone who reads this material is a Christian. If you are not sure where you stand with the Lord, please read the Appendix in the back of this book and respond accordingly. Although God loves people who don't believe in Him, He's slow to push His will on them. He gave us a free will, so He's not going to turn around and snatch it away until this test called life is over. God offers some fantastic blessings, but the price tag is that we must make Him Lord over every aspect of our life.

LOOKING FOR THE IMPLANTS

Now, let's look at some Bible verses that show that some of the destructive thoughts that pop into our head are from the enemy. When I use the term "enemy," I'm not referring to the devil, per se, but to the angels that fell from heaven with him. These are demons or evil spirits.

And another sign appeared in heaven: and behold, a great red dragon . . . and his tail swept away a third of the stars of heaven, and threw them to the earth.

Revelation 12:3,4a

This passage of Scripture is giving us information on where demons came from. They fell along with Lucifer. The devil was once an honored cherub, serving God Almighty, but pride entered the scene and caused him to be thrown out of heaven. Ever since, he's been the "mad scientist" intent on destroying everything precious to God, mainly, human beings. Demons are the "implants" that the mad scientist used on Willy and Barb. By using the word implants I do not mean demon possession, but harassment. I'll try to clarify the difference later.

The devil can only be in one place at a time, but he has his minions, the fallen angels. He is called "Beelzebub, the ruler of the demons" (Matthew

12:24). The term "enemy," therefore, can apply to this whole bunch, Satan and his imps.

God could have easily eliminated Satan when he rebelled, but instead, He retained him to do what God could never do... tempt us with evil.

*Let no one say when he is tempted, "I am being tempted by God";
for God cannot be tempted by evil, and He Himself does not tempt
anyone   ["with evil"].*

James 1:13

Why would people need to be tempted with evil? To see what is in their heart. When equipment is manufactured, engineers test the product to see how it will hold up. How much pressure and use can it withstand? The tests usually push the equipment to the breaking point to determine its limits. Satan is allowed to push us, harass us, etc., to see what is really inside us. Will we quit the minute things get rough? Will we react selfishly when certain situations arise? How do you know what's inside a person until they undergo the devil's stress tests? God won't allow the devil to push us too far, and He will provide a way of escape from all temptations (1 Corinthians 10:13).

Temptations reveal what is in our heart (James 1:2-4 and 1 Peter 1:6,7). Our enemy is a specialist when it comes to temptation. He enjoys his work. His input is the opposite of God's Word, and we are thereby presented with a clear choice. When we see where the demonic wisdom is coming from, and as we get to know what God says in the Bible, it will be easier to pass each temptation.

How could a perfect God create something as wicked as the devil? He didn't make Satan evil. When God created a creature with free will, He thereby produced something that could choose to go opposite of His nature. When God was all there was, there was no opportunity for sin to exist. Only when a second being existed, was there the possibility for "other than God" (sin) to exist.

WHO IS THE REAL PROBLEM?

Is the enemy really able to stick thoughts into our head? Isn't our brain a private place? Oh, wouldn't that be nice. If our brain was a safe place, then God couldn't be called our Refuge, our Shelter, our Fortress. No, there's only one safe place, and it's not between your ears.

The language the Apostle Paul uses in 2 Corinthians 10:3-5 puts "thoughts" and the enemy's kingdom in the same camp:

For though we walk in the flesh, we do not war according to the flesh, for the weapons of our warfare are not of the flesh, but divinely powerful for the destruction of fortresses.   We are destroying speculations and every lofty thing raised up against the knowledge of God, and we are taking every thought captive to the obedience of Christ.

Some folks tell us that there is no devil and that we are our own worst enemy. Apparently Jesus didn't agree with them. One day Peter interrupted Jesus' sermon with some faulty advice. Here's what Jesus said...

But He turned and said to Peter, "Get behind Me, Satan. You are a stumbling block to Me; for you are not setting your mind on God's interests, but man's."

Matthew 16:23

Notice, Peter's problem was what his mind was set on. But who did Jesus blame for the "input"?

Here's the problem as I see it. If the hurtful thoughts that arise in our mind are of our own making, then we're stuck with being a failure. We can try to clean up the mess after the spill, but if our own mind is producing the garbage, we're a pretty sick puppy. If the enemy is pumping the negative stuff into our mind and we ignorantly blame our self, then he gets away with murder, we are in double jeopardy, and it ends up being two against one – we're siding with God's opponent.

We will be looking at this issue of "who's responsible for most of the negative input" in much more detail because it's extremely important. But for now, let me just ask you to consider this: if you beat on yourself as being the big creep and it doesn't help, but when you resist the devil you experience immediate relief, which will you go for? If I can prove from the Bible that the enemy is behind a bunch of the hurtful stuff that flares up in your thinking, will you consider   fighting him instead of yourself or others?

Some people believe the devil only knows what comes out of our mouth; that he can't read our thoughts. Maybe so, but I'll bet some of these sincere folks have used the expression with those they are very close to: "I know what you're thinking." They weren't saying they are a mind reader, but that they can likely anticipate the typical human response to the present situation. How much more does the devil need to cause much mischief?

In a technical sense, we know a human has to have functioning, physical ears in order to hear what we say. How do spirits "hear"? They do-n't have physical ears. It is not that important that you agree with me on this point; however, I ask that you merely try fighting the next "internal" battle as though our foe could read your thoughts. Give him something to read!

Spirits are in the same dimension that our thoughts are in, the spirit world. "Among men," we cannot know another's thoughts, but notice how this verse links thoughts and spirit...

For who among men knows the thoughts of a man except the spirit of the man which is in him? Even so the thoughts of God no one knows except the Spirit of God.

1 Corinthians 2:11

Have you ever found yourself in a tug-of-war in your mind with something that obviously wasn't you or the Lord? If it was the enemy, then wouldn't they have to be able to know what you were thinking to tug against what you were thinking?

DOES COUNSELING WORK?

Counseling will not work very well or for very long if it assumes that **we** are the main source of our problems. Some counselors are totally ignorant of an active enemy pumping our brains with stinkin' thinkin'. Can you imagine the time a counselor would have with Willy and Barb? If he was unaware of the mad scientist, Serpetus, and his diabolical implants, his task would be herculean.

Parents are frequently blamed for serious problems their children manifest without looking behind the scenes for the possibility of negative enemy input. And yet, I could share many stories of how "incorrigible" kids immediately settled down when the real enemy was properly resisted. Don't get me wrong, I believe in disciplining children and brats are brats because they make some bad choices. But part of raising healthy kids is teaching them that not all the stuff that flies into their head is of their own doing and they surely are not obligated to receive hurtful or destructive thoughts.

Could some of the irritability and anger of people be instigated or aggravated by unseen tormentors? When we hear someone say, "That man was acting crazy," or that certain people are strange, they may be picking up on the activity of trouble-making spirits. Instead of being helpless when dealing with "out of control" people, we just may have some supernatural weapons.

The Bible is clearly saying that we have a real, aggressive enemy that is out to kill, steal and destroy (John 10:10), but because he's invisible, most of us totally ignore his existence. Yes, we can get overzealous in "demon hunting," but for most people, the imbalance goes the other way.

If a counselor was aware of what took place, then he could help Willy and Barb remove the implants, and then train them in how to guard against any future attacks. This is what we must do. I believe that once you see what our enemy is up to, you will be more than able to shut him down. Good feelings follow good thinking, and if we destroy the source of negative input, we will enjoy an abundance of good feelings. As we do, the presence of inner peace will make it even easier to spot the enemy's negative input in the future.

SAY NO TO BEING A CREEP!

I don't want to say without reservation that you're not a creep, but the chances are (especially because you're doing something to grow in your spiritual life) that you are nowhere near the "bad guy" that the enemy has led you to believe. But, you do have a very nasty enemy. And, he's hyperactive. Because most of us have been unaware of the extent of his intrusions, we have taken his bait and gotten into trouble. Look back at the last time you "lost it" and see if you can spot the enemy's input that triggered your improper response(s).

THE ENEMY'S TARGET — OUR WILL

The bottom line with Satan's devices is, **he must trick us into using our own will against ourselves.** If we get hooked by our adversary, the harder we pull in ignorance, the bigger the trouble we'll get into. If what I'm sharing is correct, then you can expect to be able to cut the line and free yourself from the enemy's harassment **very quickly**. You will experience immediate relief, success with mental hassles, and new vitality. If you stop beating on yourself and others, and start whipping on the real enemy (unseen), your bruises will heal, relationships will mend, and peace will come in like a flood. Joy, ah yes, precious joy is also a byproduct. I've seen this truth do in a few moments what many years of counseling only kept a bay. Don't reject counseling; incorporate the Bible's bigger picture to insure even greater success.

Is it a copout if we blame the devil for the junk that pops into our heads? Look at what the Bible has to say.

Now the serpent was more crafty than any beast of the field which the Lord God had made. And he said to the woman, "Indeed, has God said, 'You shall not eat from any tree of the garden?'"

Genesis 3:1

The first pull toward evil that the human race experienced came from the fallen being called Satan. It was **outside input** that Adam and Eve listened to and obeyed. But, it was **their will** that moved their hand to take the forbidden fruit and eat it. The exercise of **their will** got them into big trouble.

In the next chapter, we'll look more at what the Bible tells us we can do with this enemy. Get ready for some amazing results.

Remember to read through   Appendix   A on *How to Become a Christian*, if you're not sure where you stand with the Lord. This is an eternally important matter. Also, Appendix B lists New Testament verses that warn us about our enemy.

Chapter 2

TAKING THE ENEMY CAPTIVE

Once upon a time, a kindly old man named Joe, lived in a small rural town, Canine Corners. The town was besieged with wild dogs that would come around at all hours, barking, biting, killing chickens, and in general causing total confusion. The townspeople got the brilliant idea of getting a dog-catcher, and as popularity would have it, they elected Joe to be Canine Corner's first Dogcatcher.

Why did they choose Joe? Because he was gentle, kind, and wouldn't hurt a flea. Everybody in town loved and trusted Joe. He was the natural choice, or was he? Because Joe wanted to please everyone, he took the job and did his best to catch all the strays he could during the day. But, under the cover of night, Joe would drive to the edge of town and release the wild dogs. Of course he would tell them to not come back into town again, but you know wild dogs and how hard it is for them to obey orders.

The people all agreed that Joe was doing his best to eliminate the wild dog problem at Canine Corners, but things didn't seem to be getting any better. Because of certain restrictions beyond their control, destroying the wild dogs was not an option. It appeared that their only recourse was some sort of containment.

* * * *

Many believers are trying to "clean up" their lives in much the same way as old Joe. What Christian doesn't believe in demons? Yes, they can and do harass us. They need to be run out of town. Yes, amen. But, what, pray tell, is going to keep them out of town? What Joe needed was a dog pound, a jail for wild dogs. If he could but lock them up, the town would soon enjoy relief from all the commotion.

So, too, with believers. If we had a place where we could lock up the evil spirits that harass us, maybe we could get some breathing room. Well,

God has just the place – the Abyss – the spirit world's equivalent to a dog pound.

For if God did not spare angels when they sinned, but cast them into hell and committed them to pits of darkness, reserved for judgment...

2 Peter 2:4

The Greek word translated "hell" in this verse is *tartaroo*, and is used only in this verse (in the Bible). It literally means, *"the deepest part of the abyss."* God has prepared a special place of imprisonment for spirits that go too far. Look at what Jude 1:6 adds to Peter's statement:

And the angels who did not keep their proper domain, but left their own habitation, He has reserved in everlasting chains under darkness for the judgment of the great day.

According to this verse, why were some angels locked up? What do you think this means? How long were they to be locked up?

Some Bible scholars feel that this leaving "their own habitation" was none other than some of the fallen angels cohabiting with human women. Genesis chapter six, they say, refers to the angels as the *Sons of God*. The progeny of such a union, we are told, were the Nephilim, giants (Genesis 6:4 nas). The dictionary has a word to describe such an unthinkable perversion – incubus. Maybe this theory is true; I feel we don't have enough clear evidence to make dogmatic statements one way or the other. But, nonetheless, the seriousness of the sin of the angels described in Jude 1:6 was so great that God locked them up in **everlasting chains,** in His jail, the abyss. For how long?

Not all of the angels that fell with Lucifer were locked up until the final judgement – just the ones that "went too far." In the book of Revelation there is a picture of the Abyss being opened and a hoard of creatures coming out to harass the earth dwellers. These are apparently the demons that have been locked up through the years, but they are not the ones God sent there (as described in Jude 1:6) because *...He has reserved* (them) *in everlasting chains under darkness for the judgment of the great day.* The fallen angels that went too far and left their proper habitation are locked up until the final judgement outlined in Revelation chapter 20.

How did the evil spirits that come out of the Abyss during the tribulation become incarcerated? What we'll see is that some of the demons in Jesus' day begged Him not to send them there; so, He must have been sending some of the demons to the Abyss. Yes, God made a prison for evil spirits.

DEMONS ON THE LOOSE

Jesus talked about a demon leaving a person and wandering about for a while in desert places (Luke 11:24-26). The evil spirit then moseyed back to the home he left. The place was nice and empty so he took along seven bigger, meaner demons and had a "homecoming." What was Jesus' point? Don't cast out demons? I don't think so, because He had just commissioned His disciples to go out and heal people and cast out demons. Was it to teach us to guard our newly-cleansed house? Yes, but more.

I imagine this re-possessed person was as confused as the towns-people in Canine Corners. It looked like Joe was doing his job, but the wild dog problem persisted. The hope for the people of Canine Corners battling wild dogs, and we humans who battle harassing spirits, is having a place to incarcerate the troublemakers.

But if I cast out demons by the finger of God, then the kingdom of God has come upon you. When a strong man, fully armed, guards his own homestead, his possessions are undisturbed; but when someone stronger than he attacks him and overpowers him, he takes away from him all his armor on which he had relied, and distributes his plunder. He who is not with Me is against Me; and he who does not gather with Me, scatters.

When the unclean spirit goes out of a man, it passes through waterless places seeking rest, and not finding any, it says, "I will return to my house from which I came." And when it comes, it finds it swept and put in order. Then it goes and takes along seven other spirits more evil than itself, and they go in and live there; and the last state of that man becomes worse than the first.

Luke 11:20-26

In these verses, Jesus was responding to the allegation of the crowd that He was casting out demons by the power of Beelzebub (the prince of demons). According to the first sentence of this passage, how was Jesus casting out demons?

The key verse in this passage is 23: *He who is not with Me is against Me; and he who does not gather with Me,* **scatters** *(Luke 11:23).* Notice how this statement is made on the heels of overpowering demons. I think Jesus was telling the would-be exorcists (verse 19), that He didn't scatter the spirits when He cast them out, like others were doing. He and His crew bound (gathered) them and sent them to the abyss, as we'll see in Luke 8:31. When others cast out demons, they left them to wander about in desert places, resulting in a worse condition for the victim. I can't see Jesus leaving someone He ministered to worse off.

A MADMAN ON THE LOOSE

Most believers are aware that there are evil spirits that constantly harass people. They know the enemy is real. They are convinced the battle is tough. But it never dawns on them to storm the dark fortress and take the enemy captive. It's as though most believers are living before the days of SWAT teams. When they read that we are to "destroy fortresses" (2 Corinthians 10:3- 5), they think this means that we're to pray and ask the Lord to do something about the problem. But, **what if Jesus did His part and is now waiting for us to do our part?** What if He fully intends for us to use the armor and weapons He gave us? The Bible says He is sitting at the Father's right hand, waiting for His enemies to be made His footstool. What if that's our job and He's waiting on us to "tie up"the foe?

I can hear some war-torn saints praying... "Jesus, those are real bullets the devil is shooting at us." The Master replies, "Did I not give you the shield of faith and tell you it would quench EVERY fiery missile. And, My child, why did I give you a sword? To hide it in a glass case or to use it as you storm the gates of hell and set captives free?"

Making His enemies a "footstool" sure sounds different than chasing them off, only to have them show up again at an inconvenient time. If it's our job to fight this fight of faith **now**, and to "crush him under our feet" (Romans 16:20), how can we settle for just scattering the enemy like the exorcists in Jesus' day? We can't destroy evil spirits – that's God's job (as seen in Matthew 25:41 and Revelation 20:14) – but we have been given the authority to bind.

I will give you the keys of the kingdom of heaven; whatever you bind on earth will be bound in heaven, and whatever you loose on earth will be loosed in heaven.

Matthew 16:19 niv.

The New Living Translation uses the word "lock" in this verse. Sounds like we have a job to do. Revelation 9 talks about a tremendous "jailbreak" after we're out of here at the rapture; but that's after we've done our job. For now, part of our equipment is the legal right to bind or lock up the enemy. Somebody tell Mr. Joe the dogcatcher that there's a dog pound.

REAL BULLETS

As an example, let's say we're a soldier marching through the terrain of Afghanistan, and we hear the crack of a rifle and feel the searing pain of a bullet in our left arm. We fall to the ground, take our emergency first aid pack and dress our wound. We get up to move on, and, whamo. We take another round, this time in our right leg. The process continues until we run out of medical goods. Okay, so one bullet would probably finish us off, but this is the way most Christians "fight" the devil. When we're too wounded to do anything else, we reach out for help.

Wouldn't it be better, right after being hit the first time, to take the sniper out? We will spend our life patching wounds and dodging the enemy's bullets, but we can reduce the amount of enemy fire when we consistently take out the snipers. Here's the sad reality: We have "smart" weapons that know exactly where the sniper is hiding, and they always hit their target. Why don't we use them more often? It's probably because no one told us we have such weapons, nor has anyone demonstrated how to use them?

Let's replay the scenario the way it should be. We're walking the same rugged path, talking with our surveillance unit (the Holy Spirit) via our walkie-talkie (prayer). We're warned, "Take cover, inbound." We duck and hear something go buzzing over our head. We lift our rifle in the direction of the sound of the shot and pull the trigger. "Thud." We hear something fall to the ground. Yes!

When we release our "heat-seeking" anti-missile missiles, they hone in on the very source of harassment. All we have to do is release our faith by a command of authority . . .

"I bind the spirit that threw that thought at me, in the name of Jesus!"

The angels take our faith command, as a **warrant**, and arrest the spirit that shot at us! Hallelujah. We can't kill the evil spirits, but we can bind them and lock them up in the jail God uses. We can't lock up evil spirits indiscriminately any more than we can have "suspicious-looking" people arrested. But, when we catch spirits trying to push us into illegal behavior, breaking in as a thief, or seeking to put sickness on us, we have just cause for a warrant. Have you ever had the Holy Spirit warn you in advance that the enemy was throwing a temptation at you?

JUGGLING, ANYONE?

Suppose the enemy throws one thought at us. We play with it for a while, and before we get rid of it he throws another thought. Now we have two thoughts to deal with. Instead of destroying the thoughts, we ponder them both, first one, then the other. As we're deep in thought over the two temptations, here comes another inbound missile. Now we have three temptation thoughts buzzing around in our head. Let's say the process continues. Soon we're a mess. We may even think God has allowed us to be tempted above what we can bear (1 Corinthians 10:13). What is the problem and what is the solution?

For though we walk in the flesh, we do not war according to the flesh, for the weapons of our warfare are not of the flesh, but divinely powerful for the destruction of fortresses. We are destroying speculations and every lofty thing raised up against the knowledge of God, and we are taking every thought captive to the obedience of Christ.

2 Corinthians 10:3-5

What do you suppose will happen to the demons when we destroy their fortress? Don't you suppose they'll be put out of commission? Even if we chase off each temptation, we have not obeyed the Word until we have destroyed the source of the temptation thoughts – the fortress.

Wouldn't it be better to take the sniper captive and not just his fiery missiles?   We might get a little peace and quiet if there were fewer bunkers lobbing bombs at us. God didn't call us to juggle the enemy's temptation thoughts. **We've been given the authority to bind and loose; we'd better use it!**

Let's look at Matthew 16:19 again:

I will give you the keys of the kingdom of heaven; and whatever you shall bind on earth shall be bound in heaven, and whatever you shall loose on earth shall be loosed in heaven.   [Also Matthew 18:-18]

When we bind something on earth, it's bound in heaven. This is the invisible, yet very real world where Satan and his minions do their dirty work. The main Bible version used in this study is the New American Standard. Notice how the NASB renders Ephesians 6:12:

*For our struggle is not against flesh and blood, but against the rulers,   against the powers, against the world forces of this darkness, against the spiritual forces of wickedness in the **heavenly places.**   Ephesians 6:12*

If you use the King James Version, you will notice that the last line differs from the NASB.

*For we wrestle not against flesh and blood, but against princi-
palities, against powers, against the rulers of the darkness of this
world, against spiritual wickedness in **high** places. (Bold added)
Ephesians 6:12 kjv*

The Greek word translated **high** by the KJV, is EPOURANIOS. This is the
only verse where the KJV translates this word high; elsewhere the KJV
renders it: heavenly – 16 times; heaven – 1 time; celestial – 2 times.
Obviously, our wrestling match is with evil powers in heavenly places. The
word "high" might throw some off, as though the foe posed little problem
down here on earth – wrong! When we on earth (in our four dimensions)
use our authority to bind, the foe is bound in heaven, the unseen spiritual
realm where he's active.

There are a few special insights we can gather from the use of this
Greek word, EPOURANIOS. Notice what Ephesians 1:3 (KJV) says:

*Blessed be the God and Father of our Lord Jesus Christ, who hath
blessed us with all spiritual blessings in heavenly (EPOURANIOS)
places in Christ.*

The source of our spiritual blessings is in the very realm the wrestling
match is taking place. Maybe this is why we do not see as many of God's
promises working for us as we desire. Perhaps the enemy is stealing our
blessings before we appropriate them.

*And hath raised us up together, and made us sit together in
heavenly (EPOURANIOS) places in Christ Jesus.*

Ephesians 2:6 kjv

Christians are seated with Christ in the spirit world called "heavenly
places." This news changes the odds in our favor. "Seated with Christ" is a
position of rulership. And over whom are we to be ruling? The enemy is
described in Ephesians 6:12: *rulers... powers... world forces of this*

darkness... spiritual forces of wickedness in the heavenly places. We may not be able to see the enemy with our physical eyes, but we have all the power of God at our disposal with which to fight.

> *To the intent that now unto the principalities and powers in heavenly (EPOURANIOS) places might be known by the church the manifold wisdom of God.*
>
> *Ephesians 3:10 kjv*

This verse makes the inner war quite exciting. It is literally saying that Father God designed things so that His church gets to inform the devil and his angels that we have authority over them. The negative side of this is that if we don't use our authority over Satan, the job won't get done – it's our duty to bind and loose.

OUT OF SIGHT

You might be tempted to think that our task will be difficult because we can't see our adversary. After all, what if the wild dogs Joe was trying to catch were invisible? Oh, but hang on for a minute. Didn't Matthew 16:19 say that **whatever** we bind on earth **shall be** bound in heaven? Apparently, our faith commands work like a heat-seeking missile. They can zero in on the enemy, seen or unseen, and **bind** him. We only have to aim in the general direction of the temptation thought and fire. It's up to the angels to take our faith commands straight to their intended target. Glory to God.

Try this with the next negative thought that pops into your head, and tell me what happens.

> *"Spirit that threw that negative thought of_____________, I bind you in Jesus' name and send you to the abyss."*

If a thought of lust pops into my head, and I'm born again, and I don't want the filth, then a spirit threw it. We'll look at this more in future chapters. What I hope you'll see as we go through this material is that you're not the nasty old person the enemy wants you to believe you are. We make the inner war much harder than it really is supposed to be when we are ignorant of how the battle is to be fought. Most believers turn their tongue-gun on themselves:

"I'm my own worst enemy; I guess I'll never get my act together."

They flail on themselves while the enemy keeps lobbing bombs at them. Man, that doesn't make good sense: it's two against one, and they are actually working for their enemy.

Do you know anyone who's caught in this trap of beating on the wrong enemy? It's not too easy to explain to others what they're doing, without them thinking we're crazy. If we mention the devil too much, they might call for the guys in the white jackets. I get frustrated because I see what's going on, but few people will stop thumping on themselves or others and join in the task of cleaning up the area around us from the unwanted, unseen opponent.

Some Christians are smart enough to know that the inbound missiles are from the enemy, but they only scatter the snipers. Like the sons in the Luke 11 story, they chase away the demons, but scattering demons only sets the stage for massive re-attack.

Jesus' teaching also lets us know that demons like to hang around in groups. I think these rascals run in pairs or herds. One throws a gross thought at us, then another one says, *"Shame on you, you naughty boy . . . and you call yourself a Christian."* When they work us in teams, we'll lose every time unless we know what's going on. If they don't get us to take the filth, they usually can get us to beat ourselves bloody with guilt. Talk about using our will against us. Have you caught the enemy "double-teaming" you, such as putting a gross thought in your head, and then trying to make you feel guilty for having it?

CUFFING SPIRITS

We don't bind thoughts, we bind personalities – demons. Thoughts just disappear if not played with. Can you recall all the thoughts you had last week? Of course not. You only remember the significant ones, the ones you pondered and the ones you acted upon. If a thought is received, then the process of faith goes into effect. We can take thoughts captive, but if we don't obey the first part of the 2 Corinthians 10 passage and destroy the fortress, we're going to be busy taking a lot of thoughts captive.

Chapter 3

. . .AND STAY OUT!

But the Spirit explicitly says that in later times some will fall away
from the faith, paying attention to deceitful spirits and doctrines of
demons.

1 Timothy 4:1

In the last days demons will trick people into falling away from the faith. Isn't that what this verse says? If a person can be tricked by a demon into leaving the faith, then they can also be led into some serious demon control. This truth should sober us up. What I hope you can see is that demons can pose problems for believers. They **is** the enemy. (excuse my grammar). They work nonstop to poison our thinking by offering what James calls demonic wisdom.

This wisdom is not that which comes down from above, but is
earthly, natural, demonic.

James 3:15

If Jesus told His church to cast out demons, then we'd better do just that, whenever and wherever we encounter them. If a spirit is the driving force behind your inability to get out of a rut, then cast it out.

Please don't allow theology devised by the enemy to poison your thinking. Who do you think cooked up the idea that Christians can't have problems with demons? Remember, he's a liar and will twist the truth to his advantage.

"Demons? There are no demons; that's old dark-ages theology. This
is the modern twentieth century. Don't be silly."

In 2 Timothy 3:5, we're warned to avoid people who have a form of godliness but deny its power. Typically, the same people who tell us that there are no such things as demons, tell us that we don't need God's power today; after all, we have science. They are the same ones that will be quick to send you off to a secular counselor but will mock you if you mention evil spirits. Secular counseling can help if it points the counselee toward the responsible behavior mentioned in the Bible, but, without the knowledge of what's going on behind the scenes, you can't win the war.

People who ignore the reality of Satan and his demons are marching into battle with empty rifles. They will end up in a pile and then probably get mad at God because He didn't **make** them resist the devil. I'm sure all Bible-believing Christians would agree that we're to fight the fight of faith (1 Timothy 6:12). Who, pray tell, is the enemy we're supposed to fight? Surely not other believers and other denominations. We are fighting against:

...the world forces of this darkness, against the spiritual forces of wickedness in the heavenly places.

Ephesians 6:12

Some people get upset with God because He allows all the suffering in the world. What are they overlooking? The small thing called the **free will** of mankind, and the big thing called Satan and his fallen kingdom. I believe that anyone who will honestly read the Bible cover to cover, will have to agree, there are harassing, unseen spirits that we must resist in the name of Jesus if we are to successfully complete our occupation of planet earth. There is suffering because there are evil spirits and it's not God's job to do something about it—He gave the job to us (Mark 16:16,17).

THE GOD OF POSITIVE AND NEGATIVE

Some of the disturbing thoughts that enter our mind are from the Lord. From time to time He needs to bring us back from our wanderings and **convict** us of being selfish or ornery. When thoughts of conviction come from the Holy Spirit, they are filled with hope and point us toward the fountain filled with the Blood of Jesus. Behind Spirit-given "negative" thoughts is the call to get back with the Lord; to get back on the narrow road that leads to the Kingdom of God. His call reminds us of the good times, the sweet fellowship and the deep inner peace that we once had as we walked with Jesus.

If the negative thoughts that bounce into our head have no hope, only condemnation, then they are not from the Holy Spirit. Have you spotted the difference between negative thoughts that come as conviction from the Holy Spirit and the hopeless thoughts of condemnation from the devil?

Some of the crazy thoughts that bounce through our head are from our data banks, our brain's storage facility. Our mind is full of years of trivia as well as useful information. We paid good money and spent valuable time storing this information. But, along with the good data is junk – some is from us, some is from well meaning friends, enemies, and yes, you-know-who.

SHADOW BOXING?

"What if I bind a spirit and there isn't a spirit present?" This is a very good question. What is a good answer?

If I bind a spirit and "there's no one there," what have I lost? If, however, I'm attacked and the lying spirit tells me that it's just me being a creep as usual, and I buy it, I'm in trouble. Jesus said truth will set us free; buying the devil's lies takes us further into bondage.

Our authority is directed only against spirits, principalities and powers of darkness, not the good angels or people. So, fear not. When in doubt, cast it out.

[Check out Appendix B for New Testament Scriptures that point out our real enemy.]

WHERE JESUS SENT THE DEMONS

One day a crazy man loaded with evil spirits came running to Jesus. The spirits called themselves Legion. In the Roman army, a legion of troops was from 4,000 to 6,000 in number. No doubt Legion was exaggerating a bit, as is the demonic custom.

[Let me interject that this story shows that even thousands of demons can't keep someone from coming to Jesus if they **"will"** to come. Satan can't overpower our will, only deceive us into surrendering it.]

Then Luke tells us the demons did something bizarre:

And they were entreating Him not to command them to depart into the abyss.

Luke 8:31

Why did the demons ask Jesus to not send them to the abyss? Could it simply be that they didn't want to go there? Can you imagine evil spirits asking Jesus to not send them into the abyss if He had never thrown any there before? Even a simpleton would know you don't give someone an idea that you don't want them to carry out. No, Jesus was in the regular habit of destroying the works of the devil. Compare 1 John 3:8 with Acts 10:38.

But when people keep on sinning, it shows they belong to the Devil, who has been sinning since the beginning. But the Son of God came to destroy these works of the Devil.

1 John 3:8 nlt

compare with:

You know of Jesus of Nazareth, how God anointed Him with the Holy Spirit and with power, and how He went about doing good and healing all who were oppressed by the devil, for God was with Him.

Acts 10:38 nas

Jesus healed such things as spirits of infirmity and deaf and dumb spirits. He was thereby destroying the works of the devil. Fortresses were taken. I believe Luke 8:31 gives us clear insight into what Jesus usually did with the spirits – He locked them up in the abyss.

In Matthew 8:16,17, we see Jesus healing by casting out demons. Verse 17 is a quote from Isaiah 53:4, and says *"He carried away"* our diseases. Where did He carry them? You can believe what you want, but I feel Jesus healed sick people by carrying away the demons that were causing the diseases, and He locked up the offenders in the abyss.

FOUR REASONS FOR LOCKING UP THE ENEMY

1. WE ARE TO DO THE WORKS OF JESUS!

Truly, truly, I say to you, he who believes in Me, the works that I do shall he do also; and greater works than these shall he do; because I go to the Father.

John 14:12

True discipleship ordinarily requires imitating the one doing the teaching and training. Paul said:

Be imitators of me, just as I also am of Christ.

1 Corinthians 11:1

Therefore be imitators of God, as beloved children;

Ephesians 5:1

This is exactly what Jesus did. Compare these two verses:

Jesus therefore answered and was saying to them, "Truly, truly, I say to you, the Son can do nothing of Himself, unless it is something He sees the Father doing; for whatever the Father does, these things the Son also does in like manner."

John 5:19

compare with:

For if God did not spare angels when they sinned, but cast them into hell and committed them to pits of darkness, reserved for judgment . . .

2 Peter 2:4

If Father God locked up the angels that fell, and if Jesus locked up harassing demons, and we are to imitate them, then we must do the same thing.

In 1 John 3:8 we are told that Jesus came to destroy the works of the devil. To destroy is much more than just chasing away bad thoughts like Joe tried to do with the wild dogs (chapter 2). To **destroy** is putting the *source* of the thoughts out of commission.

There is a parable in Matthew chapter 22 that is a picture of the Kingdom of God. At the end of the story, the father (God) of the groom (Jesus), responds to someone who entered the marriage hall in such a way as to be offensive to the bride (us, the church). Notice what He does with the irritator:

Then the king said to the servants, "Bind him hand and foot, and cast him into the outer darkness; in that place there shall be weeping and gnashing of teeth."

Matthew 22:13

Because we are to imitate Father God as His own dear sons, we too must incarcerate harassing, side-tracking, irritating, distracting spirits that have no business polluting the holy place of our mind. We are to guard the sanctuary of our inner being to keep trespassing spirits out. Guards need to be able to makes arrests – and so do we. What has been your response to demonic harassment: Lock up the perpetrators? Chase them off (like old Joe)?   Or, ignore them?

2. WE HAVE THE AUTHORITY TO LOCK UP EVIL SPIRITS!

According to Romans 5:17b, we are to rule in life:

. . . much more those who receive the abundance of grace and of the gift of righteousness will reign in life through the One, Jesus Christ.

Do rulers have the right to take prisoners? Even small towns, if they're big enough to have a police force, are authorized to take criminals "captive." Part of ruling in life is the authority to apprehend outlaws; not just say "shoo, be gone" but to actually lock them up.

Our badge of authority is clearly seen in Matthew 18:18:

Truly I say to you, whatever you shall bind on earth shall be bound in heaven; and whatever you loose on earth shall be loosed in heaven.

3. OUR JOB IS TO SET CAPTIVES FREE:

In Luke 4:18, Jesus quoted from Isaiah and said He came to fulfill this:

He has sent Me to proclaim release to the captives ... to set free . . .

.

We, His church, were commissioned to carry out and complete what He began:

...God... reconciled us to Himself... and gave us the ministry of reconciliation.   2 Corinthians 5:18

Is this not the fast which I choose, to loosen the bonds of wickedness, to undo the bands of the yoke, and to let the oppressed go free, and break every yoke?

Isaiah 58:6

The enemy is into binding people:

*And this woman, a daughter of Abraham as she is, whom Satan has **bound** for eighteen long years, should she not have been released from this bond on the Sabbath day?*

Luke 13:16

*And they may come to their senses and escape from the snare of the devil, **having been held captive by him to do his will.***

2 Timothy 2:26

Because people are blinded and bound by the enemy, we must set them free before they can understand the gospel. Jesus said that truth will set captives free (John 8:32), so, every time the gospel is preached and the truth is received, captives are set free. The reason so few receive the truth is because they are blinded by Satan (2 Corinthians 4:3,4), and the one witnessing to them is unaware that they must bind the enslaving spirits.

Do you think there is any advantage to binding spirits when witnessing to someone?

4. WE MUST MAKE THE LORD'S ENEMIES HIS FOOTSTOOL:

The Lord Jesus is presently seated at the Father's right hand in heaven. According to 1 Corinthians 15:23-25, this dispensation will not end until His enemies are made His footstool. If Jesus is seated, and the Father is seated, whose job do you suppose it is to make the Lord's enemies (demons) His footstool? Who is told to "fight the fight of faith" (1 Timothy 6:12)? Against whom is the fight of faith?

Being a "footstool" is another way of saying His enemies are captured, tied up, rendered helpless. In war days of old, the defeated kings would be bound, thrown down at the feet of the conquering king, whereupon he would cram his foot on the neck of the defeated foe. And, hallelujah, this is our job.

And it came about when they brought these kings out to Joshua, that Joshua called for all the men of Israel, and said to the chiefs of the men of war who had gone with him, "Come near, put your feet on the necks of these kings." So they came near and put their feet on their necks.

Joshua 10:24

And the God of peace will soon crush Satan under your feet.

Romans 16:20

We're fighting the same enemy the Apostles fought, and, we have the same job description they had; therefore, we must have the same authority they were given in Luke 10:19:

Behold, I have given you authority to tread upon serpents and scorpions, and over all the power of the enemy, and nothing shall injure you.

If we don't take the Lord's enemies captive,   they won't be taken captive.

Because we've been commissioned for the "fight of faith," it's not a question of should we, but **will** we?

OLD TESTAMENT ABYSS INSIGHT

But those who seek my life, to destroy it, will go into the depths of the earth.

Psalm 63:9

Sounds like the abyss, doesn't it?   When David wrote Psalm 63, he thought his enemies were people. He sure knew where they were headed. The Holy Spirit gives us a more complete revelation of who our real enemies are in Ephesians 6:12—demons. Destination: abyss.

Son of man, wail over the multitude of Egypt, and cast them down to the depths of the earth, her and the daughters of the famous na-tions, with those who go down to the Pit.

Ezekiel 32:18 nkj

In some of the prophecies of Isaiah and Ezekiel, rulers of the physical realm were addressed as though they were in fact demonic powers. Most Bible scholars agree that these are references to the principalities and powers of darkness working behind the scenes in earthly kingdoms. The *New International Version* rendition of the above verse has God commanding Ezekiel to "consign" the hordes of Egypt to the pit. The Hebrew words for "depths" and "pit" are also rendered "dungeon" in numerous Scriptures. As with many of their prophecies, Old Testament men of God were often ignorant of the full meaning of their revelations. But, as we compare these verses with the New Testament "full" revelation, it becomes clearer that we are instructed to send the demonic powers that are working behind the scenes, to jail – out of commission.

For further study on satanic or demonic powers being referred to in human terms, see: Isaiah 14; Ezekiel 28 & 32; and, Daniel 10:13.   In Revelation 9:1-3, after the rapture of the church, we see hordes of demons being loosed from the abyss. How do you suppose they all got there?

We can chase demons away and refuse the thoughts they throw, but we can't say we've "bound" anything until the spirit who threw the fiery missile at us is out of commission.

NEW DOCTRINE?

Someone is apt to say, *"Hey, where are you getting this? I've never been told in church that we are supposed to lock up demons in the abyss? And I've been a deacon for fifty years."*

I know this all sounds too good to be true, and I'll be the first to tell you that this isn't a well-known doctrine, but it is old, old truth, and, it's something Jesus did.

And the seventy returned with joy, saying, "Lord, even the demons are subject to us in Your name." And He said to them, "I was watching Satan fall from heaven like lightning. Behold, I have given you authority to tread upon serpents and scorpions, and over all the power of the enemy, and nothing shall injure you. Nevertheless do not rejoice in this, that the spirits are subject to you, but rejoice that your names are recorded in heaven." At that very time He rejoiced greatly in the Holy Spirit, and said, "I praise Thee, O Father, Lord of heaven and earth, that Thou didst hide these things from the wise and intelligent and didst reveal them to babes. Yes, Father, for thus it was well-pleasing in Thy sight."

Luke 10:17-21

Jesus is saying in this passage (the context of which is deliverance) that these matters have been hidden from the wise and intelligent. Maybe that's why we haven't heard much about locking up spirits. But, if this information is hidden, how can one gain this knowledge? As a baby. We draw this sincere milk of the Word from the One who birthed us the second time – the Holy Spirit.

The disciples came back to Jesus (v.17) saying that demons were literally "biting the dust." Jesus as much as says, "Yes, men, remember, I said I gave you power over the enemy." When He calls them "serpents and scorpions" He's referring to the demons (like John does in Revelation 9:5). Demons are the power of the enemy. In verse 20 (same context), He calls them "spirits."

And He said to them, "I was watching Satan fall from heaven like lightning."

Luke 10:18

What was Jesus seeing in the spirit realm? A display, much as a lightning storm. Every time a demon was locked up, it was sent to the abyss, not set free to wander about in the desert. These bright lights (once stars of God, Rev. 12:4) were falling out of heavenly places (Ephesians 6:12) and hitting the earth on their way to the abyss.

In verse 18, the Greek verb translated "watching," (*etheoroun*) is in the active voice, indicating continuous action. This was a lightning storm, not a single bolt of lightning. If only Satan fell, Jesus would have said "I saw Satan fall." But, this was quite a show – many demons were being knocked out of heavenly places, and were on their way to the abyss.

Jesus thanked the Father that this was classified truth. Only childlike faith could see this. Some truth is hidden for those who are righteous (Proverbs 2:7), some for those who seek (Matthew 7:7); and some is classified until the last days (Daniel 12:9,10). I feel that the truth concerning locking up evil spirits in the abyss was hidden until this time in history, so the great end-time revival could take place (Mark 13:10). Our evangelism efforts will become progressively more effective as greater numbers of Christians get involved in spiritual warfare. After the church is raptured (2 Thessalonians 2:1,7), the abyss will be opened (Revelations 9:1-3) and the demons that have been incarcerated will again harass the inhabitants of earth in full strength.

WHAT IF YOU DON'T AGREE?

There are many "nonessential" areas of doctrine where believers don't agree with each other. Please hear me – I am not setting myself up as the final authority. If you don't agree with me on this matter of locking up spirits in the abyss, let what I say on this subject go by. Spit out what you see as bones, but eat the chicken. I will be pleased with any improvement you experience in winning the inner war; and, you don't have to agree with me on every point for that to happen. My ministry is to be like a road sign, maybe a caution sign. It's up to you to drive your car safely. You must decide how you will interpret the Word for your own personal growth.

If you don't believe in sending the demons to the Abyss, then please send them to Jesus for proper matriculation. One person told me he sent them to Africa. I freaked out. They have enough of their own problems without any help.

Also, you can safely do what Jesus did on at least one occasion – tell them not to re-enter the person. This would eliminate the problem we mentioned in Luke 11:26.

*When Jesus saw that the people came running together, he rebuked the foul spirit, saying unto him, Thou dumb and deaf spirit, I charge thee, come out of him, and **enter no more into him**.*

Mark 9:25 kjv

A CHECK LIST FOR

TAKING THE ENEMY CAPTIVE

1. At the first sign of negative thinking, **quickly draw near to God** (James 4:7,8). Pray something like this:

   "Father God, I submit to you in Jesus' name"

   By negative thinking, I mean:

   - Critical, judgmental thoughts
   - Self-righteous, proud thoughts
   - Fearful, worrisome, anxious thoughts
   - Self-hate, put-downs, failure thoughts

   - Wicked, lustful, jealous thoughts
   - Anger, hatred, unforgiveness,
   - vengeance
   - Old, hurtful memories

2. **Bind the spirit who threw the temptation thought:**

   "Foul spirit that just put that thought in my mind, I bind you in Jesus' name!"

3. **Command the spirit to go to the abyss and stay there until Jesus raptures His church** (that is, until the prophecies in 1 Thessalonians 4:13-18 and Revelation 9:1,2 come to pass).

4. **Immediately turn your focus back onto the Lord**. See Jesus, high and lifted up. Worship Him. Thank Him for saving you. Thank Him for providing the victory over the enemy (Colossians 2:15). Pray in the Spirit; praise Him freely.

   [Jesus asked us not to rejoice that we had authority over the evil spirits, but to rejoice that our name was written in heaven (Luke 10:20). This keeps us humble. Our temptation is to get too big for our britches. Whatever you do, don't get demon-minded. Give 'em a lick and get your eyes back on Jesus, A.S.A.P..]

5. **Yield to the Holy Spirit and ask Him to fill you afresh**; to control your heart and mind. A simple, yet powerful prayer is, *"Lord Jesus, please fill me and use me for Your glory. Not my will, but Yours be done in my life."*

6. **Say by faith**, *"I hate this thought of*_________________ (whatever the thought was), *in Jesus' name!"* Proverbs 8:13 says that if we fear God, we'll hate evil. We say this from our reborn spirit, **by faith**, not according to how we feel.

7. If you fell for the temptation, **confess** this as **sin** and ask Jesus to cleanse you (1 John 1:9). If there's something you need to do by way of restitution, do it.

A MUCH NEEDED WARNING

Warfare is dirty business. If you're not careful, you can spend too much time considering the negative battles that are clamoring for your attention. We need to quickly destroy incoming missiles from the enemy, bind and lock up the perpetrators, and, as soon as possible, get our focus back on positive, praiseworthy things. This process needs to become as automatic as breathing: quickly exhale the bad air, and enjoy inhaling the new, fresh air of the Spirit of God. If you bog down with exhaling, you'll soon perish. But likewise, if you fail to expel the deadly presence, you will also perish.

The mind set on the Spirit is LIFE!

Chapter 4

ALMOST UNBELIEVABLE

Aren't the crazy thoughts that pop into my head just my old nature wreaking havoc on me? Maybe not. Look at what Romans 7:17 says:

So now, no longer am I the one doing it, but sin which indwells me.

The Apostle Paul made this statement in the context of expressing his frustration with the inner war:

But I see a different law in the members of my body, waging war against the law of my mind, and making me a prisoner of the law of sin which is in my members.

Romans 7:23

This war is between what I want to do as a true believer and what sin (Satan, his demons, or my flesh) wants me to do. Despite the fact that a fight is going on in my mind, I may be just an innocent bystander and not the culprit. Romans 7:20 is much like verse 17, but it goes a bit further to give us a different slant on the inner battle:

But if I am doing the very thing I do not wish, I am no longer the one doing it, but sin which dwells in me.

How can we distinguish the difference between when it's us producing stinkin' thinkin' or when it's sin (Satan or a demon) attacking us? Most of the time sinful thoughts appear to be of our own doing, but that's not what the verses in Romans chapter seven are pointing out.

It seems like me.

I'm the one with the **feelings**!

I'm the one with the stirring inside.

Isn't it me?

Not if my spirit truly doesn't want the sinful thoughts!

Is there a part of you that wants to be holy? Do you want to please the Lord? Do you want to get the victory over sin? I'm not talking about remorse. Even criminals feel remorse, remorse that they got caught. If you truly feel bad about improper responses, not just that you got caught, but that you even had the bad thoughts, then **it's not you**! Have you felt this inner tug-o-war? Feeling that you want something wrong, but also a sense that you don't want the wrong thing?

Look at Romans 6:6 & 7

Knowing this, that our old self was crucified with Him, that our body of sin might be done away with, that we should no longer be slaves to sin; for he who has died is freed from sin.

What are these verses saying about your "old self" (sin nature)? Here's where we must go by the **fact** of God's Word rather than our feelings.

This will probably be the hardest thing for you to believe!

We must consider or reckon God's Word to be true even if our flesh says something different. This is the fight of faith and it's not always pleasant because our flesh demands that we take it seriously. But, praise God...

WE ARE UNDER NO OBLIGATION TO TAKE THE FLESH AND SINFUL THOUGHTS SERIOUSLY!

Read Romans 6:11 & 12

Even so consider yourselves to be dead to sin, but alive to God in Christ Jesus. Therefore do not let sin reign in your mortal body that you should obey its lusts.

Why would the Lord tell us to "consider" ourselves dead to sin? Is it because our old nature is really still alive and we must pretend it's dead, or is it because our old nature   is dead, but our mind has been fooled into thinking it's still alive?

*And in Him you have been made complete, and He is the head over all rule and authority; and in Him you were also circumcised with a circumcision made without hands, **in the removal of the body of the flesh** by the circumcision of Christ; having been buried with Him in baptism, in which **you were also raised up with Him** through faith in the working of God, who raised Him from the dead. And when you were dead in your transgressions and the uncircumcision of your flesh, **He made you alive together with Him**, having forgiven us all our transgressions, having canceled out the certificate of debt consisting of decrees against us and which was hostile to us; and He has taken it out of the way, **having nailed it to the cross.***

Colossians 2:10-14

What did Jesus do with the body of your flesh? Is Father God seeing you as a failure, a sinner, or as complete in Christ?

> *And you were dead in your trespasses and sins, in which you formerly walked according to the course of this world, according to the prince of the power of the air, of the spirit that is now working in the sons of disobedience. Among them we too all formerly lived in the lusts of our flesh, indulging the desires of the flesh and of the mind, and were by nature children of wrath, even as the rest. But God, being rich in mercy, because of His great love with which He loved us, even when we were dead in our transgressions, made us alive together with Christ (by grace you have been saved), and raised us up with Him, and seated us with Him in the heavenly places, in Christ Jesus.*

Ephesians 2:1-6

What is the picture God has given us concerning "where" we are right now? These verses make a strong faith statement about who we are in Jesus. God wants us to act as though the old person (who we were) is dead and gone. When "who we are in Christ" gets through to our mind, we'll enjoy greater freedom and power over sin. If, because of feelings and devil-generated stinkin' thinkin', we hang on to old failure pictures, we will, in essence, cancel out the Word of God.

Many defeated Christians are in essence double-minded. On one hand they believe the Bible when it describes salvation and God's amazing grace, but on the other hand **they can't believe what this salvation provides!**

It's easy to believe that we're a sinner – after all we've lived with ourselves all these years. But to believe that this new life, this salvation has baptized me into the death, burial, and resurrection of Christ and that now God considers me a new creature – well, that's a bit hard to receive. Especially when we seemingly still have many of the same old desires pulling at us. Yes, salvation brings a sense of cleansing and renewal, but soon there is the old tug to return to sinful responses.

We can **"feel"** the inner war; we can't **"see"** the finished work of Christ. So, the temptation is to believe our feelings before we believe God's Word.

Our enemy's whole battle plan is to trick us into believing that we're alive to sin. Our born again spirit hates sin, but the liar is telling us we really love it. If we're unaware of what's going on, we'll think we're going crazy, and we'll probably give up and get choked out by the weed-seed of life. The devil's propaganda is aimed at telling us we love sin – over and over, day in, day out. He says. . .

"I'm the problem, I'm a mess, I'm a sinner . . ." [notice, he uses the first person singular.]

WHO'S PUSHING WHOM?

As an example, let's say I'm standing next to you and I begin to push hard against your arm. But, you can't see me, I'm invisible; you only feel my pushing. If you're like most people, you'd think you were going crazy. If, all of a sudden I became visible, you would say, "Hey, stop pushing on my arm." When you could not "see" me, you would take the pressure personal.

Just because we can't **see** the imp on our shoulder, whispering his crummy comments, we usually take them as our own.

The hardest part with using our authority to bind the spirits that throw temptation thoughts at us, is not being able to see into the spirit realm to discover who is really pushing us.

The quicker you suspect the enemy for every negative thought that pops into your mind, and resist him, the faster you will enjoy the abundant life Jesus promised.

I talk to people all the time that are trying to conquer habits. They usually tell me how hard it is to quit and how they "love" the habit. Then I ask them, "What part of you wants to quit and which part of you loves the habit?" What I want them to see is that there is a part of them that wants to quit. First they tell me they want to quit the habit, then they tell me they love it. Have you ever experienced this tug-of-war over quitting a habit?

This **is** the **inner war.**   It's the "new you" versus "the flesh" (the part that opens the door to the enemy). The flesh is not the old nature or the sin nature (that died when we were saved, Romans 6:6,7). The flesh is that part of us between our five senses and our mind. Our physical body (flesh and blood) is basically neutral. For example, when the enemy pokes our hormones, our mind picks up the result as "sexual arousal" or a flesh temptation.

The appetite for food is normal and healthy. The "flesh" is seen when we feel pressured to finish off the box of chocolates.

The flesh is the enemy putting pressure on one of our physical or emotional senses.

If I bind the spirit pushing me to eat too many candies, I have resisted the flesh and the enemy. When sexual impulses suddenly manifest and I resist the "sensation" as a temptation, I enjoy immediate victory. But, here's the killer:

NOT IF I PLAY WITH THE TEMPTATION!

When my will receives the temptation, plays with it, okays it, and cooperates with it, then I have sinned. Merely having the sensation is only temptation, and not sin. This explanation may not make sense to you right now. The main issue that we need to understand is that there are two warring factions within us: the flesh and the spirit.

For the flesh sets its desire against the Spirit, and the Spirit against the flesh; for these are in opposition to one another, so that you may not do the things that you please.

Galatians 5:17

Beloved, I urge you as aliens and strangers to abstain from fleshly lusts, which wage war against the soul.   *1 Peter 2:11*

The enemy attacks our flesh (our five senses) with such things as feelings, appetites, ruts, stinkin' thinkin', etc. The untrained mind assumes that these powerful "experiences" are the old sin nature. Paul's discovery in Romans 7:20 was the good news that these feelings are merely **an assault**.

If we can retrain our mind to quickly agree with our spirit rather than our flesh, continual victory is within our grasp. We must purpose to stay on the Spirit's side. When the pressures of a conflict rise, declare, **in spite of feelings**, reasoning or any supposed evidence, that you are on Jesus' side. This frees us to push, with determination, against the evil side.

Let me say this again. In order to win the inner war, we must first agree that there are these two parts inside of us – the **flesh** [the door sin uses to access our brain – our five senses], and the **spirit**.

The next step is to side with the one we want to win. It gets tough at this point because no matter which one we side with, the other one will throw a fit. You've never heard a brat throw a screaming fit until you've denied the flesh. The kind of faith we're after must realize that this is the true fight, and then make a quality decision to go with the **new nature** – the spirit.

"Sometimes when I'm praying or even when I'm in church, the craziest thoughts bounce into my head. Why do I have such gross thoughts?"

We can't control completely what pops into our head, but we can determine what we do with the thoughts. We can learn effective ways to clean up some of the atmosphere around us, but not completely. God won't judge us for what some demon throws into our mind, but He will hold us accountable for what we do with it. Jesus didn't sin when He was tempted; but He was tempted. To be tempted is all part of the test of life. Resisting temptation is victory; yielding to temptation is sin.

If we allow the weed-seed (the devil's negative input) to choke out our spiritual life, then we're in big trouble. Especially when He's provided such excellent weed killer.

STRONG FEELINGS

Let's look at how emotions or feelings can captivate our faith:

But each one is tempted when he is carried away and enticed by his own lust. Then when lust has conceived, it gives birth to sin; and when sin is accomplished, it brings forth death.

James 1:14,15

When, according to James, does the temptation turn into sin? Do you suppose it's possible to "feel" like we've blown it, and yet, not actually pass over the fine line of committing sin? Sure. I think this happens all the time. We throw in the towel too soon. We feel the pull to sin, so we say, "Oh well, I thought it, I might as well do it." Or possibly we feel like the sinful feelings are an old friend that we can't be rude to.

Hey, wait a minute. Resist the feelings and win. Satan threw feelings of hunger at Jesus, but He didn't give in to them, or even acknowledge them. Jesus said that it's not what goes into a man that defiles him, but what comes out. Therefore, we're not defiled until we "act" upon the enemy's input.

"What's the big deal about determining who's putting the gross thoughts in our mind? If they're gross, then we must resist them anyway, so why worry about who put them there? What difference does it make?"

I'm glad you asked. If you take the enemy's assaults personal, you will develop a terrible self-image. You can be tricked into spending much time beating on yourself, and it will be a fairly simple matter for him to trick you into giving up the war as hopeless. He will even put suicide in front of you as the only option for dealing with such a crummy person – an obvious mistake of God – the whole time you are a...

BORN AGAIN,

NEW CREATURE IN CHRIST;

A VICTORIOUS SAINT,

CREATED IN THE IMAGE OF GOD;

MADE COMPLETE IN CHRIST!

Yes, it's tremendously important that you discover what Paul found to be the simple truth:

So now, no longer am I the one doing it, but sin which indwells me.

Romans 7:17

But if I am doing the very thing I do not wish, I am no longer the one doing it, but sin which dwells in me.

Romans 7:20

When we see the negative feelings, the stinkin' thinkin', the destructive reasoning, as none other than the enemy trying to come through our flesh-door, we'll get mad enough to do something about it. Like the angry Russians that revolted against the domination of cruel, wicked Communism, we too will start pushing back and using our God-given authority to clean up the area around us.

CAUTION:

Never forget that there are two immediate responses required of us when tempted: James 4:7:

Submit *to God...*   ***Resist*** *the devil.*

We must **first** draw near to God. We were made by Him and for Him. He designed us to accomplish His will, not the other way around. By submitting to the Lord first, we close any doors of opportunity to the enemy that we may have inadvertently opened by rebellion or ignorantly "doing our own thing."

Secondly, after we check in with Father God, take aim at the intruder. **The wicked, aggressive enemy that wants to kill, steal and destroy, poses as US!** He paints the word "Enemy" on our back. He slaps these phoney signs on others. Soon, we're all taking cheap shots at each other, and he slithers off to cause more havoc elsewhere. Are you tired of this?

I've said it before and I'll say it again and again. Once you've accepted his weed-seed, the sin is **yours**. We can't point to our pile of sin and say "the devil made me do it" and walk away. Once we've been suckered into taking his bait, we must **confess** the sin as ours and make proper restitution.

My hope is that we will spot the enemy's trap **before** we fall into it. I want us to stop beating on others who have taken his bait, and ourselves, and vent the whole of our frustration and anger on him – **the accuser of the brethren!**

SEVEN SIGNS THAT IT'S NOT YOU

WANTING TO SIN!

1. Is there a two-sided tug-of-war in your mind? [Romans 7:20]   Is there a part that doesn't want the sin? Then it's probably not you.

2. Does the thought seem to come out of nowhere?

3. Does the thought or feeling repulse you? [Romans 7:20   If you don't want it, it's not you.]

4. Is there a strong sense of urgency to "do something."? The devil wants us to act before we think.

5. Is there a building of pressure (anger, lust, fear, etc.), like someone's egging you on? This is weed-seed growing.

6. Is there a deep inner check that this is wrong? This is the Holy Spirit warning us. Our Guide will always give us a warning.

7. Is something telling you that you deserve this, or that you'll show somebody a thing or two, or a similar justification?

Did you notice how I referred to Romans 7:20 twice in these seven signs? It's because this verse is the key to the whole battle strategy. If you truly and totally want to sin, then you need to do something quickly. You need to be born again. But, if there is a "new you" deep inside that is sick of sin and frustrated with failure, then praise God, you are a new creature in Christ; the old things have passed away and new things have come (2 Corinthians 5:17). Your enemy has been defeated by King Jesus and it's your job to tell him so (Ephesians 3:8-10). If that new part is not there, then please turn to Appendix A in the back of this book, read it, ponder it, and ask Jesus to become your Lord and Savior.

I've been pushing faith pretty hard because it is our only line of defense as well as offense. When we come to an awesome verse like Romans 7:20, it takes faith to apply it to ourselves. What about you? Is your faith strong enough to step over the barricade of feelings when temptations assail you? Will you raise your voice above the wicked-one's and say with Paul, *"I don't want this evil thing, therefore it's not me, but Sin himself. Away from me you foul tempter"?*

Take a few minutes to think through the steps you'll take when feelings try to intimidate you into denying what God says about the new you.

AN UNANSWERABLE PRAYER

God cannot answer the prayer that pleads for no more bad thoughts to come into the mind. We would be in heaven then. We'd be un-testable. What God does answer is the prayer that asks for wisdom and skill to combat the enemy. We can't say, "Lord, take away my free will to choose to sin." We can pray, "Lord, help me catch temptation thoughts sooner."

REVIEW

We can actually lock up enemy agents that are harassing us, but first we must be convinced that the junk that pops into our head is from them, and not of our own doing. Our biggest stumbling block to believing this is what we "**feel**." The enemy tells us his lies over and over until we start to believe them. As we begin to receive his lies, he throws in a bunch of feelings as collaborating evidence. Negative-faith, combined with feelings, pressure us to act. This process produces very strong impulses and feelings. But, it's not our sin until we act accordingly. To turn this process around, we must believe God's Word more than the enemy's evidence. Sounds simple, right?

THIS IS THE BATTLE LINE!

Chapter 5

YOU'RE NOT CRAZY, YOU JUST HAVE A CRAZY ENEMY

Sin is aggressive. Notice below what God told Cain. His brother, Abel, offered animal sacrifices, just as God had directed. Because this pleased God, He demonstrated His pleasure by blessing Abel. Cain did just the opposite by insisting on offering what he wanted to offer, not what God asked for. God showed His displeasure by ignoring Cain's offerings. Cain was steamed. Then the Lord said:

If you do well, will not your countenance be lifted up? And if you do not do well, sin is crouching at the door; and its desire is for you, but you must master it.   Genesis 4:7

This is a very important truth that God shared with Cain, and we are on our way to victory when it finally gets through to us...

We humans have an aggressive foe who is always trying to trick us into using our own will against our self.

Satan's desire is to consume us, but we must master him. It's a war and it's literally a matter of kill or be killed. Genesis 4:7 says "sin" is what is trying to get us. This is an euphemism (symbol) for the devil. Jesus said the devil is the father of lies and **the first murderer** (John 8:44); therefore, this "sin" that was crouching at Cain's door was none other than Satan. The devil tricked Cain into using his will to murder Abel.

In the story of Cain and Abel, a spirit of jealousy and a spirit of murder were working behind the scenes. They were literally crouching at Cain's door. He lost the inner war by opening the door to them. He responded to the thoughts these spirits put into his mind **as though they were his own thoughts**, even after God told him that an outside force called sin was trying to master him.

Revelation 12:9 describes Satan as the one who "deceives the whole world." Our enemy does not have the authority to storm into our lives and destroy us. He must deceive us into using our will against ourselves – we must give him our authority.

...and do not give the devil an opportunity.

Ephesians 4:27b

When God said sin was crouching at Cain's door, He used the word "door" as a symbol for Cain's will. Jesus used a similar figure of speech in Revelation 3:20, when He said He is at our door, knocking, waiting for us to open up to Him. We must use our free will to open to either the Lord or to the enemy.

Satan couldn't force Adam and Eve out of the Garden of Eden. He couldn't threaten them with bodily harm if they didn't get out or pull a sword on them and demand they leave. However, all he had to do was to get them to use their will for his purposes. Satan's goal was accomplished smoothly and almost without effort by simply getting Eve to use her will to obey him and disobey Father God. His plan of attack has not changed much since then. He must trick us into action that is illegal, and such action begins with simple thoughts. He told Eve, in so many words, "You can't live without this forbidden fruit." She believed him and got into big trouble.

See if you can catch any thoughts popping into your head in the next couple of days that are telling you that you really must have something illegal... you owe it to yourself to indulge in something wrong. I'm hoping that you will get in touch with the kinds of thoughts that run around in your head, and deal with them quickly and decisively.

Detecting the enemy's lies is made more difficult by poor thinking habits. Our fleshly mind is very self-protective and self-centered and, therefore, very susceptible to the twisted thoughts that our enemy throws at us. When he appeals to our selfish flesh, he gets our attention. His "words of wisdom" make flesh-sense and they promise to feel so-o-o-o good.

DESIGNER SINS

The enemy has a full range of thoughts to trap us, depending upon our particular weaknesses. For the strong, there are **pride** thoughts: blow your own horn, and push your way to the top and step on whoever you must. For the weak, there is **fear** and **laziness**. For the curious, **gossip**. Something for everyone. Temptation thoughts have an appearance of wisdom, but they are a fleshly means to attain what we think we want or need and they lead to bondage.

The enemy can't hook everybody with violent, selfish behavior, so he cooked up **false humility** and a **legalism** that takes away everything fun. He destroys others with thoughts that they are too stupid, too ugly, too fat, too old, too young, too... What has the enemy used the most on you?

On one hand is the lure to **power** and **wealth**, and on the other hand is **false humility**, **asceticism** and legalism. Our persistent enemy will use whatever it takes to try to sneak one over on us. He may use opposite tactics back to back. One minute you may be tempted to feel that you can do anything, the next minute, your feelings are telling you that you are and always have been a failure. The bottom line is that it will take work to renew our thinking processes if we are going to win each confrontation.

Our will is very sacred to God. He won't force us to do something against our will (generally speaking); and our enemy is limited to tricking us into abusing it. Life is a series of opportunities to use our will for God's glory, to say by our actions that we love Him. When our ways please God, we're blessed. When we obey sin's impulses, we're sucked into a downward spiral of misery. No wonder our enemy is out gunning for us.

THE LURE OF LUST

This inner war can also be compared to the power struggle of espionage. Most spy stories have a handsome, good-guy agent who is seduced by an irresistibly beautiful opponent. She steals his affection, much like Delilah won Samson's heart. Satan uses the emotional pull of the love of this world and the lust for other things to invade, bind and conquer. He can come at us fighting, swinging, flinging missiles of violence, or charming us into a compromising situation. Both are deadly, but, please catch this, in both cases *he must trick us into using our will against our self.* He is not given the authority to break into our lives;   we must open the door for him.

The devil comes on to us many times like a harlot. The power of a harlot requires that her victims must believe that they need what she has to sell. If a man's heart belongs to another and his needs are amply taken care of, she cannot make a sale. We could say this woman of ill repute depends upon customers that are convinced they "need" what she has to sell. How can we fight the lies that we need something that the enemy is trying to sell us?

Sin must evoke a response from us. If we agree with it, believe it, love it, chase after it, then something is born in us – death. Two parents are required if there is to be a birth, and so it is with sin. We could say the devil is the father, offering to us a seed-thought, and we are the prospective mother.

Contrary to this, the Lord wants us to obey Him and bear the fruit of the Spirit. Whomever our mind gets involved with will be the father of our baby. But, it will be **our baby** – our responsibility.

Keep in mind that it's not a sin to be tempted. Jesus was tempted, but won each scrimmage. Praise God, we can too. We know Jesus "felt" the first temptation, where Satan suggested He make bread from stones. Jesus had gone 40 days without food and the Bible said He was hungry. When the devil said the word "bread," Jesus felt the hunger pains all the more. Just because we "feel" the temptation thought doesn't mean we've sinned. It just means that the temptation is **real**. Do you have a problem blaming the devil for temptations when you "feel" them strongly?

MORE EVIDENCE

And the tongue is a fire, the very world of iniquity; the tongue is set among our members as that which defiles the entire body, and sets on fire the course of our life, and is set on fire by hell.

James 3:6

What sets the tongue on fire? What kind of damage is done by this fire? Our very own tongue, like a gun, is pointed back at us. Ponder James 3:2-5. The tongue is mighty important; no wonder hell's out to commandeer it. Look at what the enemy is trying to sell us:

This wisdom is not that which comes down from above, but is earthly, natural, demonic.

James 3:15

The demonic wisdom this verse mentions is the logic our foe uses to trick us into believing his input. You may feel led to say, when tempted,

"That was just me," but the chances are, if it was negative, it was demonic wisdom. The following verse is from the New International Version:

The Spirit clearly says that in latter times some will abandon the faith and follow deceiving spirits and things taught by demons.

1 Timothy 4:1

How do demons teach? They don't have mouths, so how do they speak? We humans need to have a mouth in order to speak, and we need ears if we're going to hear. No, spirits don't speak out loud. Spirits communicate with thoughts, not vocal cords. That's why we must take every "thought" captive to Christ. Why would we be told to take every thought captive to Christ unless each thought could possibly be contaminated by the enemy?

For the weapons of our warfare are not of the flesh, but divinely powerful for the destruction of fortresses. We are destroying speculations and every lofty thing raised up against the knowledge of God, and we are taking every thought captive to the obedience of Christ.

2 Corinthians 10:4,5

Maybe, just maybe, we're not the big bad-guy we thought we were. Maybe we're not the "mess" the devil's been telling us we are. Have you ever heard someone say that they are their own worst enemy? Maybe they're wrong.

Here's an interesting story. One day Jesus asked His disciples, "Who do people say I am?" After the disciples gave Him the results of the latest Gallup Poll, Peter made the famous statement, *"You are the Christ, the son of the Living God."* Jesus said that Peter did not think this up on his own, but that the Father had revealed it to him. Hmm. No credit for Peter. Then, after Jesus shared that He would have to be crucified, Peter said,

...God forbid it, Lord. This shall never happen to You.

Matthew 16:22

Notice how Jesus responded to Peter:

But He turned and said to Peter, "Get behind Me, Satan. You are a stumbling block to Me; for you are not setting your mind on God's interests, but man's."

Matthew 16:23

Who did Jesus blame for the wrong response? Why was Peter's comment so bad? I imagine Peter was a bit red-faced. What had actually taken place? Satan stuck a thought in Peter's mind and Peter, without knowing what was going on, blabbed it out.

We can get into big trouble if we feel we need to "tell others what we're feeling" if the input, the feelings, are from the enemy. This is where "communication" and "expressing yourself" calls for some serious understanding and insight. If we share our perspectives with others, and these "insights" are the result of enemy input, we will find our self in a mess similar to Willy and Barb, and Peter. They thought that they owed it to themselves to express what they felt, when the thoughts and feelings were being generated by an evil, **outside** force. Do you frequently experience pressure to share what you're feeling?

We see the first couple in the Bible, Adam and Eve, tricked out of Eden by listening to the devil's lies. The first sibling, Cain, killed his brother, even after God clearly told him of the invisible war going on for his mind. Peter was embarrassed in front of the disciples because he was unaware of the source of his "insights." And, then there was Ananias.

When Ananias lied   in Acts chapter five, notice what Peter said (He probably reflected back on his own experience):

But Peter said, "Ananias, why has Satan filled your heart to lie to the Holy Spirit, and to keep back some of the price of the land?"

Acts 5:1-3

Who filled Ananias' heart to lie? What kind of demonic wisdom do you suppose the enemy used to trick him? The demonic wisdom that assails us continually "makes sense." Our problems are started, maintained, pressurized, increased, etc., by our enemy. He coaxes us into sin (like with Cain, Genesis 4:7), and does everything he can to convince us to stay there. He wants us to develop **ruts** (which makes his job easier), and if possible, to get an appetite for the particular sin, sick as this may seem.

BUT WHO GETS IN TROUBLE?

Just because the devil tricks us into sinning, doesn't get us off the hook **after** we do it. Once I (ignorantly or knowingly) obey the impulse to sin, I'm the one in trouble and I'd better repent as soon as possible and get right with God and those I've hurt. The faster the better. But, let's work on stopping the process **before** the chickens get loose.

There is a double whammy when we obey Satan's impulses. We not only fall into sin; something else takes place. Look at Romans 6:16:

*Do you not know that when you present yourselves to someone as slaves for obedience, **you are slaves of the one whom you obey,** either of sin resulting in death, or of obedience resulting in righteousness?*

When we take the enemy's bait we start towards bondage. The more we obey him, the deeper our bondage grows. This is the negative power behind habits.

Sometimes it appears that the enemy really has our best in mind, and that God just wants to spoil our fun. That's the line he used with Adam and Eve, and it's his major approach to our modern, self-centered society. If I've learned anything, it's that God is the only one without selfish or evil motives. Even the best of humans has mixed motives. God tells us over and over in His love letter to us how to maximize life, find fulfillment and overflow with joy.

Learn to question every thought that comes into your mind. The ones that are obviously good and righteous, go with. Thoughts that smack of self-protection, self-righteousness, anger, lust, pride, self-destruction, self-abasement, judgmentalism, the easy way, laziness, fear, worry, etc., **resist in the name of Jesus**. And don't forget, we're only responsible for the thoughts we take; what we act upon.

The next chapter is about good and bad faith. Once we see how our faith has worked against us, it's easier to use it to work for us to move mountains.

Chapter 6

FIGHTING STINKIN' THINKIN' BY FAITH

The major problem with fighting and winning the inner war is that the whole process works by faith. If I'm not sure I have the authority to stand up and fight, the mad dog will sense my double-mindedness and proceed to chew me up. If I don't know how faith works, the enemy will easily trick me into using my authority against myself or he'll snare me with being double-minded.

This kind of faith boils down to feelings versus faith. Is the unseen realm of faith stronger than what I can reason, see or feel? Can the simple promises in the Bible actually repel the strong feelings that sweep over me?

Feelings can come from what we focus on, can be given to us by the enemy as temptation or by God as a blessing. When we focus on sad things, we feel sad; good focus, good feelings (generally speaking). There are times when the presence of God comes with fantastic feelings—what a blessing. Our enemy, also, can throw feelings at us. Perhaps you have felt a wave of fear or depression come over you all of a sudden. I believe that this is none other than the devil tempting you with these feelings. It's a test and must be resisted in Jesus' name.

Here is a foundational truth:

God designed the entire universe to run by laws of faith, and Satan must operate by these laws as well as you and I.

GOD'S ADMINISTRATION OPERATES BY FAITH

...the administration of God which is by faith.

1 Timothy 1:4 nas

The Lord made everything **by** faith, and everything must respond **to** faith. The only way we can please God is when we operate by faith (Hebrews 11:6). The just or righteous person must "live" by faith (Romans 1:17). Without the added ingredient of love, nothing will profit (1 Corinthians 13:1-3); however, love must work by faith (Galatians 5:6).

In the Garden of Eden, Satan used basic faith principles to get Adam and Eve to fall. He didn't force them to eat the forbidden fruit, but merely gave them a suggestion. When Eve acted on the devil's word, she fell into sin. That's how simple the process is.

HOW DOES FAITH WORK?

1. FAITH STARTS WITH A WORD-SEED.

The Bible says faith comes from a word. Jesus likened the process to a farmer sowing seed. God's kind of faith comes when the Holy Spirit sows a word from God in the field of our heart. The devil's kind of faith starts when one of his imps whispers some weird thoughts into our mind.

God made words and thoughts to be vehicles for releasing and transporting faith. For instance, in Romans 10:17 we are told that *faith comes by hearing and hearing by the Word of God.* **Faith travels upon words.** If I speak God's promises to myself over and over, they begin to build faith inside my mind. If I allow negative words to run around in my head, they'll produce negative, deadly faith; the kind that says, "Why try, things aren't going to get better."

I caught a phrase sneaking into my noggin the other day... "I'm getting maxed out." I had a lot to do and this thought popped into my head to try to make my job harder. I noticed an increase in my energy level as I came against this enemy seed-thought.

Have you caught any negative thoughts running around in your head that drain your energy, make you angry, lonely, etc.? Words are powerful. The wrong words can make a person give up trying. Good words can give new hope. God used words to create the universe. Romans 4:17 tells us how God operates:

...God, who gives life to the dead and calls into being that which does not exist.

Look at this astonishing verse . . .

Death and life are in the power of the tongue, and those who love it will eat its fruit.

Proverbs 18:21

If our mind is the battlefield, then words are the weapons. You-know-who loves to use them to drain us, pain us, and reign over us.

WEED SEED

Jesus gave a parable one day (Matthew 13) about four different responses to God's seed. If God works by faith, and if faith works by word-seeds, then this parable is very important for us to consider.

The first response some people have to God's Word is to **ignore** it. Jesus said that when this happens, the devil, like a bird, swoops down and snatches away the seed. Maybe you reacted this way before you were saved. You turned the TV dial and came across a Christian program. The preacher said, "If you don't repent, you'll perish." You said, "Naw, that's crazy," and turned the dial. The "Naw, that's crazy," was a negative-faith seed stuck into your brain by a spirit assigned to keep you from getting saved. You obeyed the thought (without even thinking) and thus you released the negative power of faith.

SURFACE SALVATION

The second response people have to God's Word is to receive it, but only **superficially**. Jesus called this "rocky places." We might say the person has a "hard head." They will not give serious thought to God or His promises. Jesus said that when these people encounter afflictions or persecutions because of the Word, they fall away. He's not saying that trials kill their good seed, but that their shallow involvement with the Word is the problem.

I've seen this response in so many people. They pop into church when their life is crashing. They reach out to God for a quick fix. They're really not interested in corrective surgery, only a bandage and an aspirin. How about some deep-cleansing salvation? "No thanks, just get this pain to stop." Well, his wife forgives him and takes him back in, or he finds a new girlfriend. The emergency is over and all it takes is the slightest wind and "poof," their new faith is history.

SINCERE, BUT TOO WEAK

The third response to God's word-seed is to receive it and give the **appearance** of really growing, but, bad company derails the train.

And the one on whom seed was sown among the thorns, this is the man who hears the word, and the worry of the world, and the deceitfulness of riches choke the word, and it becomes unfruitful.

Matthew 13:22

The key word is "choke." The person's faith is too weak to fight the negative input because of a lack of exercise and nourishment. What two extremes, according to Matthew 13:22, will choke out the good seed of God's Word?

If your mind is always full of the devil's weed-seed, there won't be much room left for God's faith-seed. Too much bad news preempts the good news. Too much TV, playing or pampering the body, weakens the spirit and thus helps the determined weed-seed to accomplish its goal— choke out the Word. Old friends or habits make for rough growing for newly planted Word-seed.

Which of these things (last two paragraphs) do you feel will pose the greatest danger to God's faith-seed in your life? When Jesus told this parable of the four responses to the Word of God, He was not implying that there was something wrong with the Word. Each of these attacks on the good seed is what I've been calling stinkin' thinkin'. Satan's job is to get us to believe something other than God's Word. His weed-seed has to work by faith. If we can spot his weed thoughts **before** we act on them, our battle is more than half over.

A little later in the same chapter (Matthew 13), Jesus said:

The kingdom of heaven may be compared to a man who sowed good seed in his field. But while men were sleeping, his enemy

*came and sowed tares (weeds) also among the wheat, and went
away.*

Matthew 13:24,25

What do you think Jesus' point was in these verses?

2. THE FAITH-SEED MUST BE RECEIVED!

For seed to do anything, we must receive it. We do this by pondering
on the seed-thoughts. Contemplation is powerful because it causes a
word-seed to begin to germinate. This is how a general promise from God
is changed into a definite, specific promise for us. It is also how the
temptation process builds up steam.

We must play with a thought in our mind to make faith begin. A person
doesn't run out and have an affair the first time the devil throws kinky
thoughts into their mind. No, the process starts slowly, through pondering
on the temptation. The same is true with positive faith. We don't, all of a
sudden, flex our spiritual muscles and move a mountain by faith. Faith
needs to grow. **Our faith is watered by what we focus our mind on.**

*For the mind **set** on the flesh is death, but the mind **set** on the Spirit
is life and peace.*

Romans 8:6

The word "set" is pondering, meditating, mulling over something.
When we want this process to work miracles in our life, we must ponder
on God's promises, His good faith-seed. What kinds of things do you catch

yourself pondering the most? How easy is it for you to meditate on God's positive promises?

FIELD OF THE HEART

The place where the Word germinates is our heart or as the world calls it, our subconscious mind. Our subconscious mind picks up what we are mulling over during the day. As our conscious mind ponders, stews, chews on something, it slowly trickles into our heart or the subconscious portion of our mind.

Jesus said that what comes out of our heart (subconscious mind) can defile us. I believe it's because this is what will control us. When the chips are down, we will act upon what our heart believes. Can you see how this thing builds? What we ponder on trickles down into our subconscious mind, and then we actually begin to believe it. We make our choices (or responses) based on these conclusions in our heart.

Bad conclusions = problems!

Good conclusions = success!

Resolve and faith emerge from our pondered conclusions – sometimes this all takes place at the subconscious level.

This whole process gets even more scary as we consider the mind/body connection mentioned in Proverbs 23:7:

For as he thinks within himself, so he is...

Isn't this verse saying that we will become what we think? If we think sick thoughts, we'll become sick. If we think gloomy thoughts, we'll become depressed. If we ponder angry input, we'll become angry. Our deep, inner faith will create the physical reality. These are physical reactions to what a person is thinking. We could say that the enemy is using the laws of faith to kill people with stinkin' thinkin'. When we receive his thoughts (faith weed-seeds), something starts happening.

On the positive side of this truth is what Proverbs (chapters three and four) says: health, healing, and even wealth comes from meditating on and obeying the Word of our God. Read these chapters and note the power that is available by studying, believing and obeying the Word.

REPETITION IS POWERFUL

In World War II, a technique was developed called "propaganda." The power of propaganda was always around, but Hitler honed it into a very forceful and destructive tool. If told a lie enough, the people will believe it. Modern ad agencies build their campaigns on this principle. They bombard us continually with sales pitches for their products. Hitler was able to get otherwise sane people to destroy their fellow human beings by this form of mind-control. Madison Avenue is trying to get into our pocketbooks with this tool.

Behind the law of propaganda is the truth that we will begin to believe what we hear over and over. This is why someone who has heard all their young, impressionable life that they are stupid, ugly, etc., will believe it even in the face of contrary evidence. The deeper, subconscious mind actually can believe untruths if told over and over, and if given half a hearing. What makes it worse is if there is some negative evidence, such as the kid who has their normal shortcomings pointed out as evidence of being a failure. Do you know anyone who has a bad self-image because of this law of repetition being used by the enemy?

We can see how this law of repetition works to destroy, but God gave this law to protect and equip us with mountain-moving faith. In Deuteronomy 6, He told us to use this faith-building concept in training our children. Tell them the truth of God's Word over and over. What we are doing is helping them **ponder** God's promises.

3.   POWER IS RELEASED WHEN WE ACT ACCORDING TO WHAT WE BELIEVE.

I have talked to many men who feel strong love for their wives, but their wives complain that their husbands don't care about them. They frequently tell me that the romance has left their marriage. Some even say they feel "used". Why the difference of opinion between what the husband says he feels and what the wife says she senses? The difference may be because there is little or no corresponding action on the husband's part.

Faith without corresponding actions is dead.

James 2:17 (Paraphrase)

The most powerful "corresponding action" to God's good seed is praise. When we give thanks in advance, we are operating by faith. Some people feel that if they speak something positive before they can see it, they are lying. But, follow them around and listen. Before long, they will speak some negative weed-seed that is not yet a reality. "I just know I'll get caught in a traffic jam," or "I'll probably get a cold and it'll ruin my vacation." They can speak of things that are not, just as long as they are negative. Now, who do you suppose is behind that one?

God's corresponding action when He created the universe was speaking. This is how He operates, and we are told to imitate Him as His children (Ephesians 5:1). Pay close attention to this verse:

...God, who gives life to the dead and calls those things which do not exist as though they did.

Romans 4:17b nkj

When we praise God that His promises are true, **before** we **see** the answer, we are releasing the same powerful faith that God used to make everything we see. When you claim a promise from His Word, immediately begin praising Him for the results. See it as done. Praise soaks the good seed in nutritious, living water. Praise is the best corresponding action I know of. How often do we pray and ask God for something, then turn right around and destroy our faith-seed by bad speech? Why is it so hard to speak positive things and so easy to confess negative junk? I suppose we have help.

4. A FAITH-SEED MUST GROW UNTIL IT PRODUCES FRUIT!

In the Matthew 13 story, Jesus said that it was only that which went all the way to fruit that was considered productive. When the seed was choked out or snatched away, the intended goal was not reached. This is exactly what I want us to do with devil-sown seed thoughts: **destroy them before they bear fruit.**

You've no doubt seen this process work on someone. They are upset and stewing over something. They may even be muttering about it. After a prolonged time of meditating on the anger thoughts, they explode and throw a fit. The weed-seed was nourished until it bore fruit. If we don't defuse the time-bomb of stinkin' thinkin', it'll blow up inside us.

My point is that if we can catch what's going on, even though we **feel** anger, lust, fear, etc., we can stop the process before we actually sin. When we bear the fruit of what we've been meditating on, then we're in trouble. Once we actually sin, then we must **confess** our sin, **repent**, and **get right** with the Lord. But, it is possible to stop the process **before** it goes all the way. Hopefully, we'll learn how to stop the process before it gets started.

Chapter 7

INCREASING YOUR BEATING AVERAGE

Is the title of this chapter a typographical error? Not this time. I'm concerned about one of the enemy's slick techniques – discouragement. His bag of tricks is limited, and the more we know how he works, the better advantage we'll have.

Basically, he tells us that we are not presently batting a thousand, so, we'd better quit. When you slip up and allow some of his missiles to get by, and perhaps blow up at someone, or pamper your flesh, his henchman says, "You'd better give up. You'll never make it. Save your energy."

Have you experienced this temptation?   I'm sure we all have.

Have you noticed how the enemy avoids you when you're hot, but when your resistance is low, he gets all his buddies to "jump you"? What do you expect? He's in this thing to win (he still thinks he can.). Fully expect his worst attacks when you're down – flu, headache, low on the Word, surrounded by company, picked on by mean people, etc. And, as soon as you succumb to his harassment, expect to hear him start singing, "You Ain't Never Gonna' Make It," followed by a chorus of, "You Might As Well Quit Now, You Imperfect Old Thing, You." Ugly songs indeed.

The good news is, we're not going by our perfection, but Jesus' perfection. And, we're here to improve our beating average. In this classroom of life, it's not how perfect I am (for none of us are), but am I growing? What steps am I taking to grow? Am I trying to learn? We've beat the enemy before; we'll beat him again.

But in all these things we overwhelmingly conquer through Him who loved us.

Romans 8:37

But thanks be to God, who always leads us in His triumph in Christ . . .

2 Corinthians 2:14a

The Word sees us through the eyes of faith. This should give us the confidence to relax and let the Holy Spirit guide us through the land mines of life, fixing our eyes on Jesus, the Author and Developer of our faith.

INCREASING YOUR BEATING AVERAGE

The title of this chapter is a play on the familiar phrase, "Improving your batting average." But this is not about how many times you strike out when you're playing baseball; rather how frequently you beat up our deceptive foe. What our enemy fails to tell us when he says we're not batting a thousand, is that even major league ball players don't bat a thousand. They don't even come close to five hundred. Imagine, these guys get paid millions of dollars to strike out most of the time. Shoot, you do at least that good with the enemy, right?

For a righteous man falls seven times, and rises again, but the wicked stumble in time of calamity.

Proverbs 24:16

Don't listen to the accuser when he tells you you're never going to make it; rather, quote this verse:

Do not rejoice over me, O my enemy. Though I fall I will rise; though I dwell in darkness, the Lord is a light for me.

Micah 7:8

I feel that we learn a little by our successes. We're prone to believe that we've made it by some inherent goodness of our own, or because we're from good stock, etc. But, when we mess up, if we learn why we messed up, correct the situation, and then succeed, we're more humble and prone to give God the glory—plus, we've grown.

This life is all about growth; about learning. We can learn before we mess up (hallelujah) or after (hopefully). The more we meditate on the Word of God, the faster our growth, and the greater our beating average. Have you been more concerned with a perfect beating average or growth? It's hard to be a perfectionist and a human. A shift in focus from perfect success to growth will improve our attitude as well as our beating average.

SOME TRICKS OF THE TRADE

An illustration I've used before when talking with folks who feel that their authority against the devil isn't working very well, is about a car parked on a hill. Let's say it's your car, and you happen to leave it unlocked. The enemy, prowling around seeking someone to harass, reaches in to your car, takes it out of gear, and releases the emergency brake. Your precious car accelerates down the hill. If no one is able to jump in and apply the brakes, then rest assured, there is always a bottom to every hill. Hey, what's a little fender damage? Hopefully, no one was at home when the car crashed in through the front window.

My point is, you may apply the insights from these chapters too late. If you bind the enemy after he's done his dirty work, you may miss him. He may be long gone, and the momentum of his temptation will carry the event until it crashes. We can't wait until we hit the wall and then go to binding or loosing. Authority released too late will be ineffective. Instead of bemoaning our poor timing, we'd do better to install a "Holy Spirit Surveillance System" for the next encounter. When the thief has done his damage and split, yelling louder will not help – discussing the situation with our Master is the smartest response in such cases.

Meditating on the Word, praying in the Spirit and constantly praising the Lord, keeps your car locked. When you feel the slightest slipping, immediately bind the one playing with your brake. If you wait too long and get into trouble, don't give up. Spend more time with your Coach and get a new game plan.

Have you caught the enemy's trick too late, yet you tried to bind him, found nothing happened, and therefore concluded that it doesn't work to bind him? What can you do to increase your sensitivity to his "hit-and-run" tactics? How about some spiritual exercises:

PUSH-UPS?

We can learn something from the world of professional sports, where only the best win. If you want to be a winner, stay in shape. The pros can goof off and beat the average Joe, but if they want to beat the best, they pay a big price. They watch their diet, exercise, study their competition and get all the advice they can from the best trainers. Can we do less for the prize of the high calling in Christ?

Being part of an active church family and support group can stimulate your faith and pick you up when you're not feeling your best. We're not competing against other believers; they're on our team. Practice together and share insights and new techniques. It'll improve everybody's beating average.

EVERY CHANCE YOU GET PRACTICE!

For the pros there's batting cages, simulators, driving ranges, and even video assessment. For the believer, there's physical symptoms, feelings, and people. Some of the harassing situations of life are really putting greens in disguise.

Physical infirmities, disasters and irritations, are allowed by God, I believe, to be a proving grounds for miracles by maturing our faith. The mountains are in our path to make us strong (Matthew 17:20), not to mock us. The enemy derides us with, "That mountain will never move." He's right if we stop. But, if we keep pressing in, keep sharpening our faith-skills, the mountain will be moved, even if merely shovelful by shovelful.

Physical sickness is against us. It's our adversary. Therefore, when you experience the slightest twinge of pain or even a remote hint of sickness, turn your faith guns on the one who wants to "steal, kill and destroy" (John 10:10a). More likely than not, someone delivered the symptoms; send the delivery boy to jail. If you win an instant victory, hallelujah. Sing and shout and give God the glory. If not, stay in attack mode, beef up your artillery and send for reinforcements. The battle's not over until heaven; then the enemy is thrown in the lake of fire (Revelation 20:10).

You know of Jesus of Nazareth, how God anointed Him with the Holy Spirit and with power, and how He went about doing good and healing all who were oppressed by the devil, for God was with Him.

Acts 10:38

Who, according to this verse, did Jesus heal? Right, those oppressed by the devil. Most likely not all sickness is from devilish oppression, but those who were so harassed were healed by our Lord.   Some believers are drawn into controversy about whether sickness is of God or the devil. Don't waste your time arguing about this one. Read John 10:10 and Revelation chapters 21 and 22. Who wants to kill and who wants to do away with sickness?

As I see it, sickness can have two major values for believers:

1. As a warning - 1 Corinthians 11:29-32, and

2. To refine our faith - 1 Peter 1:6,7; James 1:2-4; Hebrews 12:1-13

Don't let the accuser put condemnation on you for any sickness that isn't healed or any mountain that won't move. Improve your beating average. If you can't get a sickness healed, you can at least lock up every demon that tries to put condemnation on you concerning the sickness. That could amount to quite a few in a days time. Do you consider it a lack of faith to use medical help along with prayer and faith or do you see it as a wise battle strategy?

STRESS: THE ONLY MUSCLE BUILDER

The world sure has been harping about stress. They call it a killer, a robber, etc., and even try to pin down the causes. But, I have yet to read the first article that pins the rap on our ugly enemy.

There is good stress. In fact, **God intends all stress to be good**. If we refuse to be anxious about anything, and instead cast all of our cares on Jesus, we will grow. Notice how a tree in a desert can prevent the stress of drought:

How blessed is the man who does not walk in the counsel of the wicked, nor stand in the path of sinners, nor sit in the seat of scoffers. But his delight is in the law of the LORD, and in His law he meditates day and night. He will be like a tree firmly planted by streams of water,   which yields its fruit in its season and its leaf does not wither; and in whatever he does, he prospers.

Psalms 1:1-3

What it is that keeps the tree from withering when the strong desert winds (stress) blow? Where it draws from. The first part of the passage warns against drawing from the world: wicked, sinners, scornful (mockers). The blessed, fruitful tree runs its roots over to the river and drinks more when the winds howl. The tendency is to draw sympathy from people, most of whom don't know where the living water is. To increase our beating average we need to direct our roots (focus) deeper into God's awesome promises.

The fastest way to build muscles is with resistance exercises – stress. Progressive weight lifting or exercise equipment causes stimulation of muscle fibers; the result is growth.

Consider it all joy, my brethren, when you encounter various trials, knowing that the testing of your faith produces endurance.

James 1:2,3

In this you greatly rejoice, even though now for a little while, if necessary, you have been distressed by various trials, so that the proof of your faith, being more precious than gold which is perishable, even though tested by fire, may be found to result in praise and glory and honor at the revelation of Jesus Christ;   1 Peter 1:6,7

God fully intends that tough times make our faith tougher. He oversees the "workout," and He's not a mean coach. When we **first** sense stress building up, if we quickly turn to Him, with praise, He'll give us all the grace we need to "get pumped." Faith muscles grow when exercised. See every irritation, every problem, every test as a faith workout. Find some good promises verses and soak, like an athlete drinking a protein shake during their workout.

STAY TEACHABLE

If life is a classroom, then keep learning. Learn from your enemies, from your friends, learn from the world by constant dialogue with the Holy Spirit. Learn. When you're successful, ask the Lord why. When you miss the target, ask the Lord why.

When seasons of refreshment come and the enemy slips in one of his, "Oh, think you're special, getting this fine treatment when poor people are starving in Somalia," pull out your bat and improve your swing. When he tells you that something bad must be coming your way, because things have been going too smoothly, see him as a golf ball and knock him into the (black) hole (abyss).

When you hear of some new research on the causes or cures for a disease, ponder with the Paraclete (a name for the Holy Spirit) to see if there is a parallel in the spirit realm. Try to make everything in your life bend around the Word of God, rather than the other way around. When science suggests something contrary to the Word, reaffirm what the Bible is saying. On the rare moments when the world's system agrees with the Scriptures, give all the glory to God. Because life is a classroom, make everything teach you something.

RESULTS

As your beating average increases and you clean up the atmosphere around you by locking up enemy snipers, you will notice:

1. Longer seasons of peace without mental and emotional hassles.

    Have you noticed this yet?

2. The enemy will get more subtle. Where he once used straight fear, now he may resort to logic. Self-righteous thoughts may replace old self-hate and pity-poor-me thoughts. Don't be fooled. If it's negative; if it takes your mind off the Spirit, blast it away.

3. You will no doubt let your guard down after a while and you'll wake up to the same old attacks. I don't believe these are the old demons free on bail, but new ones that must be dealt with quickly and decisively.

In the spirit realm we may have "kick me" signs on us that tell the foe that we have particular ruts. Maybe a running file is kept by the enemy on each person so new recruits from hell can pick up where the old ones left off. Who knows? They are at least as smart as flesh and blood enemies.

4. Demonic spirits are very limited as to how they can harass us if we are saved, walk in holiness, and if we act in firm, decisive faith (2 Timothy 4:18). They know if we're walking the fence, if we're feeding our fleshly lusts, if we're double-minded, and if we're not

sure we have any business binding them. [See the story in Acts 19:13-17]

5. It may seem like a lot of work to take every negative thought (and its sender) captive, but you will enjoy the fruit very soon. Dealing with the little foxes will allow the vine to produce tremendous fruit.

    Catch the foxes for us, the little foxes that are ruining the vineyards, while our vineyards are in blossom.

    Song of Solomon 2:15

6. For serious mental confusion and depression that does not respond to binding and loosing, see a Christian counselor or pastor. But first, make sure you're honestly and sincerely following the steps outlined in each chapter.

7. The healthiest mind is one filled with the Word of God, thankfulness and continual communion with the Lord Jesus.

This is a mind ruled by love, flowing with mercy and operating in faith. Such a continual flow will wash out   alien intruders immediately, and not even miss a lick. Because love covers a multitude of sins (1 Peter 4:8), we'll stay clean. We'll get hooked on holiness and eating the fruit of righteousness. What a way to go.

Chapter 8

CONQUERING CURSES

When you are constantly being pestered by life in general; when the harder you try, the behinder you get, suspect the working of curses.

Our **first** response when hard times hit should be to pray and seek God. If He reveals any sin in our life or if we've left a door open to the enemy, then we must quickly repent. When we feel the pressure to sin or beat on ourselves, we must go into action against the evil principalities mentioned in Ephesians 6:12. But, what if you do all these things and everything still goes wrong? Suspect that curses are at work.

There are several kinds of curses:

1. Legal curses (triggered by disobedience)

2. Broken covenant curses (includes covenants inaugurated

by others)

3. Hand-me-down curses (weed-seed planted by others)

SOME CURSES WORK ON A LEGAL BASIS

The first curse in recorded history was the one God placed on whomever would eat the fruit of the tree of the knowledge of good and evil. Don't eat the fruit and everything will be okay;   eat the fruit and die. A person always knew where they stood – they either had eaten or had not eaten. The curse had a legal right to destroy the transgressor, **yet it was powerless against the law-abiding citizen.**

Several thousand years after the Garden of Eden incident, the Lord listed pages of curses that would come on those who broke His laws. God let Moses know that the curses for disobedience were aggressive; they would "come upon you" (Deuteronomy 4:30; 28:15) if you sinned. I get the picture of the curse tracking down the transgressor.

When we do certain "illegal" things, like getting into pride or harboring lust thoughts, we actually give the enemy a legal right to take us to the cleaners. Scripture warns us not to give him an opportunity (Ephesians 4:27). Satan is the one who gets to test believers to determine their quality, and he loves his work. Notice what he did in Luke 22:31a:

Simon, Simon, behold, Satan has demanded permission to sift you like wheat...

Peter had sounded off with pride that he would never deny his Lord. Enter the sifter. The tester gets to see how serious our pride statements are. This is a very good reason to avoid pride. Also, we're told that God has to resist the proud, so when we're being shaken down by the devil for pride, God doesn't give us grace to resist the enemy. Time to repent.

I believe that when this kind of curse is acting against us, if we diligently seek the Lord, He will reveal to us where we sinned. He may use a preacher, a TV program, a friend, an article we read, a dream, or any other of a thousand things to show the tender heart what door of opportunity was left open to the enemy.

Like a sparrow in its flitting, like a swallow in its flying, so a curse without cause does not alight.

Proverbs 26:2

A curse without cause won't alight or work because there is no legal basis for it to work. As a policeman can't give a speeding ticket to someone driving at the speed limit, so a curse for breaking a law or a covenant can't come on someone who is a law keeper or faithful to a covenant.

What is the agent that carries out the dirty work of enforcing a curse? Is it demons? Probably. It might be something inside of us, like our subconscious mind, but regardless of who or what carries out the destructive work of a curse, **it can't be stopped by binding or loosing.**

Knowing what you do about our aggressive foe, do you think he will back off when he doesn't have to?

THEREFORE, KEEP THE DOOR SHUT!

WALK IN OBEDIENCE!

When our opponent has the upper hand legally, don't expect any mercy. We can pray and plead, but the only way to close the door of opportunity that we opened by our disobedience is through repentance, confession, and receiving the cleansing grace of our Lord Jesus Christ (1 John 1:7-2:2;   2 Corinthians 7:9-11). Binding with dirty hands won't work.

Someone might say, "But didn't Jesus take the curse of the Law on Himself to free us from the curse?"

Christ redeemed us from the curse of the Law, having become a curse for us –   for it is written, "Cursed is everyone who hangs on a tree" in order that in Christ Jesus the blessing of Abraham might come to the Gentiles, so that we might receive the promise of the Spirit through faith.

Galatians 3:13,14

Yes, Jesus took the legal curses of the Law upon Himself, so that we might escape the death and destruction that sin produces. Notice, however, that this only works for the one operating by faith. The whole universe was created by God's faith, and it must also work by faith. The laws concerning curses and blessings also work by faith.

...and whatever is not from faith is sin.

Romans 14:23b

Therefore, to one who knows the right thing to do, and does not do it, to him it is sin.

James 4:17

When we try to see how much we can get away with, we actually slip into sin and out of faith. If this were not true, a believer could live any way they wanted and suffer no ill effects. We know that's not the case.

The picture I see is that we Christians are like a person living in a submarine, passing through the sea, the sea being the destructive, aggressive forces of the world. When the saint acts in disobedience or unbelief, he punctures the wall of the sub. How much water rushes in depends on the size of the puncture. Some sin can kill us (1 John 5:16,17), some weakens us (1 Corinthians 11:29,30), but all sin hinders our prayers (Psalm 66:18).

A PATCH KIT

We've been talking about curses that come from walking in disobedience. When we walk in love (1 Corinthians 13), and obedient fellowship with our Lord (1 John 1:5-7), the door is tightly closed on our enemy and, harassing spirits **must** obey our faith commands. Flowing in love and mercy acts like a patch kit when we unintentionally sin (puncture our sub) – see 1 Peter 4:8 and James 2:13. Living the Spirit-filled life takes care of legal curses, but, there are other types of curses that can work on sincere, obedient believers.

BROKEN COVENANT   CURSES

When someone in authority over us or in our lineage sets in motion a curse, it can affect us, even if we are ignorant of it. For example, Joshua uttered a curse against anyone who would try to rebuild the city of Jericho.

Then Joshua made them take an oath at that time, saying, "Cursed before the Lord is the man who rises up and builds this city Jericho; with the loss of his first-born he shall lay its foundation, and with the loss of his youngest son he shall set up its gates."

Joshua 6:26

Though hundreds of years passed by, this curse was still able to carry out its destruction. It didn't matter if the person rebuilding Jericho was ignorant of the curse – it still worked. Read 1 Kings 16:34 to see what happened.

Jacob inadvertently released a curse against his own beloved wife, to her destruction. Jacob rounded up his entire family, possessions and work-force and snuck away from his father-in-law's compound. He did this because he did not trust his father-in-law (Laban) and feared that he would trick him into staying when God told him to return to the land of promise. Jacob and his crew had only gotten a few days out when Laban caught up with him. Not only did Laban feel that Jacob's secret departure was rude, he, in anger, reported that someone had stolen his idols. Jacob's hasty reply proved his sincerity and innocence, yet it doomed the culprit – his wife.

"The one with whom you find your gods shall not live; in the presence of our kinsmen point out what is yours among my belongings and take it for yourself." For Jacob did not know that Rachel had stolen them.

Genesis 31:32

Unknowingly, Jacob cursed his wife with death. Before his trip home ended, his favorite spouse died in the throes of childbirth.

And it came about as her soul was departing (for she died), that she named him Ben-oni; but his father called him Benjamin.
Genesis 35:18

BROKEN COVENANT

King David found things going roughly and suspected something amiss. As he sought the Lord, it was revealed that his predecessor, King Saul, had afflicted the Gibeonites, in violation of a treaty made centuries earlier. This story shows us that there is a way out of curses that result from broken covenants, but it requires hearing from God and renegotiating. David sought God first, then the made a new covenant or deal with the Gibeonites.

If we enter into a covenant, and the vow is broken, the consequences of the covenant are activated – **unless a new covenant is negotiated**. Basically, God had David renegotiate a covenant with the Gibeonites. Seeking the Lord will usually result in finding a solution that will alleviate the broken covenant curse.

If you suspect a curse is working in your life, check first through your memory banks. Did you ever make a "foxhole" vow to God? Did you make a promise to the Lord when you were young, and you failed to keep your word? What about religious relatives that may have dedicated you to God like Hannah did with her son in 1 Samuel 1:11? If a parent set you aside for special service before the Lord, you may have to do some readjusting of your vocation or do some serious renegotiating with the Master.

A twist of traditional curses is seen when Jesus said that man's traditions can make the Word of God of no effect (Mark 7:9-13). Silly doctrines concocted by our forefathers, can make it very difficult for us to flow in spiritual freedom, and in effect, can leave us high and dry when we're supposed to be walking in God's abundant promises. This is why some folks have such a hard time with healing and the full gospel message. It will require time with the Master and His Word to break such stifling curses.

HAND-ME-DOWN CURSES

Some of the most powerful curses are passed on to us by those who love us the most – our parents. Some parents may not act too fond of their kids, but most love their offspring in spite of what they convey or what is misconstrued (with you-know-who's help). Out of frustration or ignorance, some parents say things that become haunting curses. They probably hoped their words would chide their children into compliance or prompt maturity; however, too frequently their slogans became a sentence or irritant that produced the wrong fruit.

When someone says...

"You're just like your father"

"You're stupid"

"You're lazy"

"Can't you do anything right?"

"Boy, you sure are clumsy"

"You'll never make it!"

"Cancer runs in our family"

"You're a pain in the neck."

"I never wanted you"

"Why can't you do as good as your . . . "

. . . they have sown weed-seed that can grow into a nasty curse. There may be some truth to what the curse giver sees in the victim, or they may be parroting phrases passed down from their parents. Siblings pick up digs from other kids and throw them at their brothers or sisters. These put-downs don't need to be true in order to work because they're weed-seed and if told enough, they will start to work by the mere power of repetition. Somewhere along the line, the lies (curses) are assumed to be true. This negative use of faith takes great work and understanding to break.

THE DEADLINESS OF FALSE CURSES

I think that each of us knows innately that a curse without a cause will not alight (Proverbs 26:2); therefore, our typical response is to refute baseless curses. When a bratty brother says, "You're dumb," the standard response is "am not!"

Frequently, the temptation is to **prove** the curse-sayer wrong. If the unfounded curses thrown at us were ignored, I think they would quickly die. But, here is the dig, because we know the curse is false, we tend to resist the curse and we can easily slip into two dangerous positions:

PRIDE & JUDGING

If the "am not" is shot back in self-defensive pride, we're in big trouble. "I'll show you" can trigger the negative power of pride.

When pride comes, then comes dishonor . . .

Prov. 11:2

Pride goes before destruction, and a haughty spirit before stumbling.

Prov. 16:18

And something few realize, God resists the proud (James 4:6; 1 Peter 5:5). This is not a place where we want to be. We need the Father's grace and power, so humility is the smart way to go. But true humility is not agreeing with what a mean person says, but rather not trying to prove them wrong. Truth will be proven by itself; we don't need to fight for our own ego's sake. Let the Lord defend your ego.

When we get mired down in trying to "prove" we are not as dumb or bad as some antagonist says, we lose focus. Remember the huge trick of the enemy – the mind on the flesh is death.

JUDGE NOT

Most people know the gist of Matthew 7:1,2 – if we judge others, we'll be judged. If I say that the person who told me I would never make it is cruel, then every one of my acts will be judged for its cruel-ness. That's not something frail humans need to contend with. Whatever I sow, I will reap, **even if I do it out of self-defense!** That's why Jesus told us to return good for evil. Giving people "a piece of my mind" or setting them straight, sows weed-seed, and goodness knows we don't need a field of weeds in our own backyard.

When I return a curse of anger to someone for cursing me, I plant anger seed. The law of sowing and reaping insures an ugly crop is "in the mail" for little old me, the hapless victim. Our enemy loves this law of sowing and reaping, and he legally uses it to bury believers. God designed the law of sowing and reaping to be an easy way to bless us; and to reserve the blessings for those who deserve them.

REPETITION AS A NOOSE

In the worse-case-scenario, the **power of repetition** is employed by the enemy working through ignorant people. If an authority figure in our life repeatedly speaks a curse over us, and we agree with them, we can actually release our faith to empower the curse. The weed-seed produces a crop without a legal basis, yet it's licensed by our faith. These curses, I believe, make way for some very big demons. This is what I feel is going on with people who have a terrible self-image, or suffer from strong emotional problems.

Tell someone they're fat (to keep them thin), and if it backfires, they will become anorexic. They can look into a mirror, and instead of seeing the actual emaciated reflection, they only see ugly fat. I feel that this is the process that produces many of the personality quirks that sideline God's people.

"Reverse psychology" is used to make a kid try harder, stay thin, be humble, etc., and because it's not God's method for child rearing, it produces death. The Bible wants parents to sow life-giving seeds in the garden of their child's mind, but not false compliments such as "Oh you are so awesome, so perfect." We need to show appreciation when they do good. When you can't honestly give compliments because of bad behavior, share the positive   promises of God's Word with them – not preaching but rather obtainable blessings.

Planting weeds with good intentions still grows weeds. Reverse psychology is a no-no. And telling children they are doing good when they are not builds a false foundation. Better to hold the Father's fantastic promises out in front of them.

A BETTER WAY

If we resist curse input, we chance becoming judgmental or prideful (defensive); agree with it and you've licensed the destroyer to bruise you badly. Help. What are we to do? Look at these two verses:

Bless those who curse you, and pray for those who spitefully use you.

Luke 6:28

Bless those who persecute you; bless and do not curse.

Romans 12:14

The Word of God is asking us to go exactly opposite of our natural tendency. What kind of logic do you think the enemy will pump into our minds to keep us from obeying these verses?   "I can't let them get away with this." A very noble hook the adversary uses to draw us into fighting curses is, "If I let them get away with this, they'll do it to someone else." What the foe doesn't tell us is that as long as we return evil for evil, we spread the disease of the curse. If we want to stop the plague, we must return good for evil. We must overcome evil with good.

Do not be overcome by evil, but overcome evil with good.

Romans 12:21

One day Jesus passed a fig tree and, because it did not have any fruit on it, He cursed it. The next day, the disciples noticed that it was dead. In this story Jesus gives us a few details concerning curses.

The first thing we see is that a curse has to work by faith. The victim of a curse has to believe that it's true. Our legal-minded enemy is more than commodious when it comes to presenting partial, distorted evidence. In this story, we learn that it wasn't even the season for figs (Mark 11:13), which means that   curse doesn't require all the facts; merely a sliver of truth. You can't expect a fig tree to bear figs out of season, but you have to admit that it was a fig tree. That's all it takes.

This is not a story to present values of morality or fairness; Jesus is teaching Peter things concerning faith. The bottom line, in the flow of the context of the story, is that a curse operates in the faith realm. We know that faith comes from hearing (Romans 10:17), and Ecclesiastes tells us that **unless we hear the curse, it won't hurt us:**

Do not pay attention to every word people say, or you may hear your servant cursing you!

Ecclesiastes 7:21 niv

People can say all kinds of things about us and it won't hurt us unless we hear it and respond improperly. The enemy tries his best to get some-one to "enlighten" us on how others have cursed us. Then, our foe uses the law of repetition, pumping our head full of the curse, as though it were a broken record. If we're in the habit of taking every thought captive to Christ, this trick won't bear fruit against us.

FORGIVENESS AND CURSES

What does a curse have to do with forgiveness? Jesus ends this teaching vignette by admonishing the disciples to always flow in forgiveness:

Whenever you stand praying, forgive.

There is an old saying that the remedy is not far from the malady. I believe that the truth concerning forgiveness is Jesus' hidden cure for a curse. If we are to overcome evil with good and return a blessing for a curse, then we need something to empower us to be able to muster up a blessing. The only way I know to cut the tug-of-war rope of curses is with forgiveness. When we forgive, we're freed from getting involved with the curse, which would result from either resisting or receiving the curse.

When we return a blessing for a curse, we tap the power of the law of sowing and reaping, and we get our socks blessed off.

Do not be deceived, God is not mocked; for whatever a man sows, this he will also reap.

Galatians 6:7

The law of harvest is that you plant a little, and get a bunch back. Plant one grain of corn and you get a stock with perhaps three ears of corn, each containing hundreds of new seeds. When I sow love instead of hate, I will harvest a hundredfold of love. When I return evil for evil, I will get a hundredfold return on the evil I give. This law works either for us or against us, and it works for everyone regardless of who they are.

The law of sowing and reaping doesn't give discounts for those who are "getting even" because we are forbidden to touch revenge:

Never take your own revenge, beloved, but leave room for the wrath of God, for it is written, "Vengeance is Mine, I will repay," says the Lord.

Romans 12:19

Let me share a little insight that I believe the Lord gave me that can help us return good for evil...

IT'S OK TO BLESS

1. When we return blessing for cursing, we tap into the law of liberty (see James 1:25; 2:12,13).

2. When we bless, we use Romans 8:6 for our good.

3. If, perchance, we've misunderstood the person who we think cursed us, our blessing will provide mercy for us. Misjudging others heaps misjudging on ourselves.

4. Mercy will keep us teachable and produce growth in our life.

5. We avoid the emotional drain of trying to prove that we're right (tug-of-wars are lots of work.).

6. It's easy to slip into praise and worship from giving a blessing. Can you imagine how hard it would be to return a curse to someone and then switch immediately into praise for our Lord?

7. Don't worry, if the person who cursed you is unworthy of your blessing, it won't stick. Check out Matthew 10:13.

FOUR POINT

"HAND-ME-DOWN CURSE"

BLASTER PLAN

This plan of attack works. When a curse bounces around in your head (either from childhood or of recent), quickly go into action:

1. Forgive the person. Add, *"for they know not what they do"* because little do they realize that they are going to receive a hundredfold return on the weed-seed they're sowing.

2. Speak a blessing to them, regardless if they are present or not. We're returning a blessing for the evil, and if the whole scenario takes place in our mind, then that's where the blessing takes place.

3. Make the blessing something that you would like to have come back on you a hundredfold.

4. Slip into praise. Get your eyes back on the King of kings and Lord of lords. The mind set on the Spirit is life and peace.

Don't forget that if we've knowingly or unknowingly opened the door to the enemy by disobedience, we must go through the steps of repentance and obedience. Legal curses do not respond to the same treatment as do hand-me-down curses, and broken covenant curses will require special advice from the Lord. Spend some time reflecting on your life to see if any curses have been put on you. If you spot any, try this four step anti-curse plan.

It's so vital to remember that a curse without cause won't stick. So please don't give curses any glue. Avoid pride, judging and returning evil for evil. Mercy triumphs over judgement.

Chapter 9

BRING ON THE POWER

The inner war is a bit draining, isn't it: checking out our thoughts, being on guard against the enemy's subtle attacks, binding demons. Have you been tempted to forget the whole thing and go back to your old ways? Don't feel alone; that too is one of Satan's common tricks. Have you experienced any relief from the inner war by binding the spirits that throw harassing thoughts at you? I hope so. The hassle, after all, is only what we've given in to all our life. **Now that we're fighting, it just seems like more of a big deal.** Keep up the diligent fight and it will soon be worth it all.

And let us not lose heart in doing good, for in due time we shall reap if we do not grow weary.

Galatians 6:9

Have you come to the place where you can see the value in taking every thought captive and binding harassing spirits, but you realize that you still need more power? Maybe you are at that point in your spiritual pilgrimage where you really care about pleasing the Lord, but you keep falling back into old patterns.

One of the false hopes we humans have is that we will mature to the point that we will not be hassled anymore. We are tempted to think that one of these days we should be able to stand on our own two feet and not have to be crying out to God every time we turn around. Read John 15:5, and tell me if this (last sentence) is a proper response.

I am the vine, you are the branches; he who abides in Me and I in him, he bears much fruit, for apart from Me you can do nothing.

John 15:5

The Apostle Paul waded through this confusion about maturity and the reality of the inner war in Romans 7:18-24. "Won't I ever get to the point where this war stops?" Probably not this side of heaven. It's not just a matter of our "growing up," because we have a nasty, persistent, subtle enemy.

We can gain much relief by consistently locking up the spirits that attack us. Remember our dogcatcher a few chapters back? His task of catching and impounding wild dogs should get easier the longer he faithfully does his job. Yet, one of his duties is to **always be on guard for strays.**

The battle should be getting easier, but this alone will not necessarily make life more enjoyable. Getting the enemy off our back is only part of our pilgrimage; finding the abundance Jesus promised is the more exciting portion.

Joy, expectancy, looking forward to each new day, having fun, laughing, feeling close to friends, enjoying our God. These things come from something other than winning the inner war. They are fruit that results from a vital, powerful relationship with the Holy Spirit.

But the Helper, the Holy Spirit, whom the Father will send in My name, He will teach you all things, and bring to your remembrance all things that I said to you. Peace I leave with you, My peace I give to you; not as the world gives do I give to you...

John 14:26,27a nkj

These things I have spoken to you, that My joy may remain in you, and that your joy may be full.

John 15:11 nkj

Until now you have asked nothing in My name. Ask, and you will receive, that your joy may be full.

John 16:24 nkj

That He would grant you, according to the riches of His glory, to be strengthened with might through His Spirit in the inner man, that Christ may dwell in your hearts through faith; that you, being rooted and grounded in love, may be able to comprehend with all the saints what is the width and length and depth and height; to know the love of Christ which passes knowledge; that you may be filled with all the fullness of God.

Ephesians 3:16-19 nkj

One day as Jesus preached in the temple, He said something very unusual:

If any man is thirsty, let him come to Me and drink. He who believes in Me, as the Scripture said, "From his innermost being shall flow rivers of living water." But this He spoke of the Spirit . . .

John 7:37-39a

I don't know if water bubbling up inside you has much appeal, but what the Lord is saying is that the Fountain of Life, the Holy Spirit, wants to manifest His power **inside you.**

The picture of flowing water was an Old Testament symbol for the refreshing power of God. The prophet Ezekiel had a vision of the latter days when the glory of God, pictured by water, would begin to flow (Ezekiel 47). The desert would be watered and begin to produce abundant fruit. The bitter salt waters of the ocean would turn sweet. The trees that drink up this water (a picture of believers) would have leaves and fruit that produce healing.

This flow is called the "River of Life" (also seen in Revelation 22:1). I believe this is the same river Jesus was telling the people about in John 7:38 – the flow of the Holy Spirit. As water to a parched desert, so the Holy Spirit is to our soul. Jesus said of the Spirit (John 6:63a:):

It is the Spirit who gives life; the flesh profits nothing;

Need more life? You only need more of His flow of Living Water. Need more power? When Jesus was about to leave His disciples, He promised to send equipment that would meet every need; a Guide that would take them exactly where they were needed; and, a vital relationship with One called a "paraclete" or Comforter – the Holy Spirit, living inside.

For God has not given us a spirit of timidity, but of power and love and discipline.

2 Timothy 1:7

Who couldn't use some more power, love, discipline? When the Holy Spirit moves, things happen. In the Old Testament, when the Spirit came on a little boy named David, he stood up to a sassy giant, Goliath, and experienced victory. Samson was the strongest man that ever lived because the Holy Spirit would come upon him. In the New Testament, when the Holy Spirit came upon folks, people were healed, demons shrieked and fled. Great miracles abound when the Spirit is moving. Awesome love flows from the Spirit. Tremendous peace surrounds, secures and satisfies via the Holy Spirit.

The third person of the Trinity works with us depending upon what's going on inside our mind. We can quench Him or increase His flow of living water:

Let no unwholesome word proceed from your mouth, but only such a word as is good for edification according to the need of the moment, that it may give grace to those who hear. And do not grieve the Holy Spirit of God, by whom you were sealed for the day of redemption. Let all bitterness and wrath and anger and clamor and slander be put away from you, along with all malice. And be kind to one another, tender-hearted, forgiving each other, just as God in Christ also has forgiven you.

Ephesians 4:29-32

Notice the things in this passage that can quench (decrease the power of) the Holy Spirit in our lives. These are the kinds of things the enemy throws into our mind as stinkin' thinkin'. When we take his thoughts and act on them, the Holy Spirit backs off the flow of living water.

Rejoice always; pray without ceasing; in everything give thanks; for this is God's will for you in Christ Jesus. Do not quench the Spirit;

1 Thessalonians 5:16-19

Happiness, rejoicing and thankfulness are associated with the flow of the Holy Spirit. God wants us to experience an abundant life, to enjoy every day (except for the brief episodes of beating up the enemy), and to sweeten the lives and situations around us. He wants us to enjoy the Christian life so much that He sent His Spirit to provide the power.

HOW DO WE RECEIVE THE HOLY SPIRIT?

We are "born" of the Holy Spirit when we're saved:

Jesus answered, "Truly, truly, I say to you, unless one is born of water and the Spirit, he cannot enter into the kingdom of God. That which is born of the flesh is flesh, and that which is born of the Spirit is spirit. Do not marvel that I said to you, 'You must be born again.'"

John 3:5-7

However, you are not in the flesh but in the Spirit, if indeed the Spirit of God dwells in you. But if anyone does not have the Spirit of Christ, he does not belong to Him.

Romans 8:9

We have the Holy Spirit at salvation, but we do not receive His **power** ministry until we are baptized or immersed with Him. Yes, He's present in every Christian, but there's much more to His ministry. Jesus breathed on His disciples the evening of His resurrection and said "Receive the Holy

Spirit" (John 20:22). This, I think, is when they were saved. He then told them to wait in the city until the Holy Spirit was poured out on them with power (Luke 24:49; Acts 1:4-8). Did they have the Holy Spirit? Sure, Jesus breathed the Spirit into them. But there was something more that they needed

P O W E R !

In Acts 8:14-17, a bunch of Samaritans were saved through the preaching of Philip. He baptized them in water, and then Peter and John came up from Jerusalem to check things out. Yes they were born again but they needed the power of the Holy Spirit.

What about you? Are you sure you're born again? Have you experienced the baptism of the Holy Spirit as folks did in the book of Acts? If you have, then you know what I've been describing: love, peace, joy, power. You've tasted these things. But, there is the matter of stinkin' thinkin' that the enemy wants to use to quench the Holy Spirit and thus reduce the flow of His divine life in us.   Have you noticed a reduction in the flow of the Holy Spirit in your life?   If so, it's time for a refreshing.

Let's shift gears right now. If you have never received the baptism of the Holy Spirit, then this is the next very crucial step in your spiritual life. You can put it off, but you will be like a car being pulled by a team of mules. The church has crippled along through the ages, letting the devil beat their brains in, fighting fellow believers instead of demons, and for the most part totally ignoring the power of the Holy Spirit. At the turn of the century some "hungry" believers found out that the Bible still means what it says. They asked – they received. The baptism of the Holy Spirit hasn't passed away; people just stopped seeking.

THE PRINCIPLE OF FLOW:

God works with a very simple principle:

**Power flows into an area of need when it is drawn
by faith.**

In 1 Peter 5:5, we read that God resists the proud and yet gives grace
to the humble. The proud person says, "I don't need you, God." The
humble person calls out to God with all their heart – "Please help me Lord,
or I'll never make it." One He lifts up, the other He has to push away.
Why? God's power flows into an area of need when faith begins drawing.
Here's what the Lord says:

*For thus says the high and exalted One Who lives forever, whose
name is Holy, "I dwell on a high and holy place, and also with the
contrite and lowly of spirit in order to revive the spirit of the
lowly and to revive the heart of the contrite."*

Isaiah 57:15

*"For My hand made all these things, thus all these things came
into being," declares the Lord. "But to this one I will look, to him
who is humble and contrite of spirit, and who trembles at My
word."*

Isaiah 66:2

Jesus said that He only came for the weak, the sick and the lost. Why?
Because they were the ones who knew they needed Him. His power flows

into the place where needy faith is pulling. **God's miracle power does not, however, flow into needy people that are not operating by faith, otherwise, there would be no needs on earth!** We'd be in heaven. No, His power flows where it is wanted, where it is requested, where the dry, thirsty heart pulls and draws, and operates within the biblical guidelines for faith.

In the story of the woman at the well (John 4), Jesus said to her that if she would ask, He would give her living water. Asking is how we start the flow of power into our weakness. But, the flow only enters weak places.

Do you see your need of the Holy Spirit or are you still trying to fix your own life? Are you able to "get your act together" by yourself? If so, then you're not empty enough. When you cry out in the words of John 15:5, "Without you, I can do nothing," then you're getting mighty close. Paul cried, "No good thing dwells in my flesh," and thereby began making a vacuum for the Spirit to flow into.

Are you afraid of becoming a fanatic? Total abandonment to the Holy Spirit means that He gets His way, His will. Are you so dry that you'll pay any price for the Living Water? Do you want His peace and joy to the extent that you'll surrender any habit, any activity, any opinion or "right" that He puts His finger on? We may not have to give up anything, but **we must be willing to give up everything** to trigger His divine flow.

Some folks feel that God is a crutch for weak people. They, sad to say, will never know the power and life that we're talking about, unless they see the error of their stinkin' thinkin'. A grown man told me recently, with tears in his eyes, of the awesome experiences he's had since the Holy Spirit filled him. He did drugs for many years, but, he said, "the Holy Spirit is the greatest high I've ever had, and I haven't come down yet." The Holy Spirit isn't a crutch, **He is our Life!**

Stay needy. Cry out in faith to the One promising to pour out living water on the dry, thirsty land. Are you thirsty? Are you dry? He knows your need, but He's waiting for your prayer of faith. Listen to the Words of Life:

Now suppose one of you fathers is asked by his son for a fish; he will not give him a snake instead of a fish, will he . . . If you then, being evil, know how to give good gifts to your children, how much more shall your heavenly Father give the Holy Spirit to those who ask Him?

Luke 11:11-13

Ask and you shall receive. He's saying our asking starts the flow because it's a declaration that we're needy.

What was the sin of the folks at Laodicea (Revelations 3:17,18)? They said they didn't have any needs and the Lord said He was about to spit them out of His mouth.

I've talked to many people who've experienced serious problems. Some have gone through years of therapy and counseling. Some have been suicidal. Every time the Holy Spirit falls, things are changed, dramatically, and immediately. One lady tried to kill herself when she was a teenager. Subsequent attempts were also unsuccessful, but each had landed her in the hospital. As an adult, she was constantly plagued with suicidal thoughts. She asked for prayer and when the Holy Spirit fell,   she was a new woman. She told me, years later, even after having gone through very serious marital problems, that she was never bothered with suicidal thoughts again. The Holy Spirit did in a few seconds, what no one else had been able to do.

AN INVITATION TO THE SPIRIT

If you're seeking the baptism of the Holy Spirit (or if you need a "refilling") get alone with the Lord and run through these simple steps. This is merely a checklist, not a legalistic formula:

1. Are you saved? If you're not sure, please review the Appendix in the back of this book and seek the Savior until you're certain.

2. Come before the Lord in the name of Jesus. After you submit to God and draw near to Him (James 4:7,8), resist the devil: "Satan, flee in Jesus' name."

3. Ask the Lord to search your heart for any sin, stubbornness, bad attitudes or habits that need to go.

4. Wait as quietly as possible. When God puts His finger on something, don't argue with Him—yield it up.

5. Go through this "waiting & surrendering" until you **feel** clean and totally yielded. I know this is subjective, but you should feel clean after you take a bath, right?

6. Ask the Lord to fill you with the Holy Spirit (or to refill you). Ask Him to take over every cell in your body, every portion of your mind, and to totally saturate your spirit.

7. Begin to praise Father, Son and Holy Spirit. Thank Him for everything you can think of: old, new, good, bad, people, places, things, etc.

Praise until you sense the Holy Spirit joining in with your praise. Keep the flow going; let it increase. See the Lord Jesus, seated on His throne next to Abba, pouring out His Spirit on you. Draw in the Living Water as dry, thirsty land.

The angels that surround God's throne sing continually "Holy, Holy, Holy" – join them. Yield up every fear, every concern, every goal, everything you hold dear. Worship Him as your All-in-all. Soon the Spirit will be flowing. You'll know by the gusher that it's His Living Water. If syllables or sounds that don't make sense come to you, offer them up in this stream of praise. Praying in tongues is simply worship that bypasses our mind; tune out the mind, tune in the Spirit. Because you're in His presence and you're yielded up to Him, He'll keep you from error.

TO STAY IN THE LIVING WATER,

STAY YIELDED!

Remember, the thief will come to steal the good seed immediately after it is sown. He will say you faked it, your's was not a language, it was stupid. He will try to make you feel embarrassed, ridiculous, etc. Don't let the enemy steal your blessing. Run him off.

Check the fruit:

Did praise and yieldedness bring you closer to the Lord?

Did you sense His presence?

Was there peace and settledness?

Did you sense joy and love?

Did you feel like Jesus was your everything?

Praying in the Spirit is like everything else in the Kingdom of God; **there are two parts: God's and ours!** If He inhabits our praise (Psalm 22:3), then praise is required for Him to inhabit. He provides salvation, yet our tongue is needed to receive salvation (John 1:12 and Romans 10:9,10). The Holy Spirit provides the language (of men or angels, 1 Corinthians 13:1), but we provide the voice, the breath, the saying of the language.

What He puts in, we speak out. Don't wait for Him to "force" you to speak; He's looking for your cooperation.

When in doubt if a syllable or sound is from Him, speak it out. Remember, you have yielded yourself up to the Living God and are therefore vulnerable to Him, not the deceiver. If you were doing this to show off in front of a bunch of people, then you would be open to a deceiving spirit of pride. But, when you're all alone, and when your desire is the New Testament experience outlined in the Book of Acts, you need to count on the protective ministry of the angels of God. Reread Luke 11:11-13, and know that Father God will not mock your sincere request.

Chapter 10

THE POWER OF THE TONGUE

Our enemy watched as God Almighty formed the planets by His Words. Spellbound, Lucifer marveled as the sea teemed with life, vegetation appeared on the desolate surface of the earth, and animals "popped" into being as God spoke. If anyone knows the power of words, it's the fallen cherub, Satan (Ezekiel 28:12-19). In fact, it was his feeble attempt to imitate God by using speech, that got him thrown out of heaven (Isaiah 14:12-14).

There's power in words:

Death and life are in the power of the tongue, and those who love it will eat its fruit.

Proverbs 18:21

Our words can save us:

If you confess with your mouth Jesus as Lord, and believe in your heart that God raised Him from the dead, you shall be saved.

Romans 10:9

Our words can condemn us:

For by your words you shall be justified, and by your words you shall be condemned.

Matthew 12:37

This being so, it's more than obvious why our enemy is so concerned with controlling our tongue:

*And the tongue is a fire, the very world of iniquity; the tongue is set among our members as that which defiles the entire body, and sets on fire the course of our life, and **is set on fire by hell.***

James 3:6

The Scriptures warn us frequently to watch what we say:

Let everyone be quick to hear, slow to speak and slow to anger.

James 1:19b

From the fruit of a man's mouth he enjoys good...the one who guards his mouth preserves his life; the one who opens wide his lips comes to ruin.

Proverbs 13:2,3

The words that come out of our mouth are very important; however, I think there are other words that are even more critical – the words that are spoken in our mind. The words that run around in our mind will sink down into our heart (our subconscious mind). There they will begin the faith process we looked at earlier. The words that linger in our mind and heart will produce great faith or foul pollution.

If we carry on a conversation with the enemy, stinkin' thinkin' will soon result. If we talk freely with the Holy Spirit, life will spring forth. The words that fill our inner person will emerge with life or death consequences. Notice what different people in the Bible talked about in their mind:

Then Abraham fell on his face and laughed, and said in his heart, "Will a child be born to a man one hundred years old?"

Genesis 17:17a

The fool has said in his heart, "There is no God."

Psalm 15:2

...that evil slave says in his heart, "My master is not coming for a long time..."

Matthew 24:48

I believe that the inner war is made immensely harder because of "self-talk" that goes unchecked, as well as valuable "self-talk" that goes unsaid. It's easy to pick out faulty inner speech in the verses above. Abraham took up the taunt that Satan stuck in his mind, and thus shrank in faith. The fool is merely pondering the polluter's filthy blasphemy. Even laziness is a result of inner talk: "there's too much to do," "I'm too tired," "I'll do this later," etc.

Contrast what Psalm 15:2 says about the righteous person:

He who walks with integrity, and works righteousness, and speaks truth in his heart.

When we're engulfed in conflict with the enemy, our words take on vital importance – everyone knows that; **but, what is being said in our minds before conflict arises, when we're experiencing one of those brief seasons of calm, can determine who wins the next conflict, and many times, if there will even be a conflict!**

There are some vital ways we can use the power of the tongue to insure simple, quick victory and remain in the midst of the River of Living Water:

Praise and give thanks

Talk the Word over with the Lord

Pray in the Spirit

Give yourself faith "pep talks"

FRUIT INSPECTION

How can we tell if we're being controlled by the Holy Spirit? Jesus said that whatever fills the heart will come out the mouth (Luke 6:45), and "by their fruits you will know them" (Matthew 7:16).

While Peter was still speaking these words, the Holy Spirit fell upon all those who were listening to the message. And all the circum-cised believers who had come with Peter were amazed, because the gift of the Holy Spirit had been poured out upon the Gentiles also. For they were hearing them speaking with tongues and exalting God.

Acts 10:44-46

In the book of Acts, when people were baptized with the Holy Spirit, they spoke in tongues, a language they didn't know. To some, it sounded like gibberish, and they mocked saying the disciples were drunk (Acts 2:13). But, speaking in tongues was given by the Holy Spirit as the sign that He's in control. Our mind doesn't understand the language, but it makes sense to the Spirit.

After you pray for the baptism of the Holy Spirit, you may feel something bubbling up from your innermost being, as Jesus said in John 7:38, or you may find strange syllables forming in your mind. Let it out. The Spirit's part is to give us the words (or the syllables), our part is to say them. Speak it, release it. Step back from having to be in control and give yourself totally over to the Holy Spirit.

I don't want you to "fake" saying weird sounds, but I do want you to let go and allow the Holy Spirit to rise up and take over control of your tongue and your life. I believe that when you're lost in high praise, the Holy Spirit will supernaturally take over your control center, and you'll find yourself praising in a language you never learned. It's beautiful. Let it flow.

Some say this is too mystical or emotional. No, it's not mystical, it's spiritual, and, yes, it's emotional. Hallelujah! God-given emotions.

The flesh is at war with the spirit, and therefore listens to demonic wisdom that tries to deny the Holy Spirit access to the tongue.

Some people worry that they might be deceived if they open themselves up too much. What I'm suggesting is opening yourself **only to the Lord God Almighty!** I think He's big enough to stand guard, lest we be tricked when we're vulnerable. Most humans regularly open up to the enemy and close to the Spirit. Our mouths have been used far too much for griping, accusing, mocking and unbelief. Isn't it time we give the Spirit equal time?

If you're motivated by fear of being too vulnerable, you probably need to read back over the chapter on binding the enemy. Lock up everything that's harassing you. Then, surrender your mind, your speech control-center, your tongue – everything – to the Holy Spirit.

A SIDE TRIP

I don't mean to digress and slip into justifying my position on tongues, but I feel strongly that there has been too much non-biblical, bad press about this link-up with the Holy Spirit. Most people are totally ignorant about tongues, including Christians. I know a little bit, but I've studied tongues extensively and paid a big price to find out what I do know. I only ask that you read what I have written with an open mind. Ask the Lord if this is true. Examine the Scriptures to see if this matches up with our **only** rule for faith – the Bible.

More is written in the New Testament about speaking in other tongues than there is about the Lord's Supper, water baptism, the Trinity, or many other important doctrines. Yet some people say tongues are of the devil or that they've passed away. Why? Could it be that there is power in speaking in tongues, so the enemy has to do something to stop it? He'll try to get us either fighting tongues or into pride that we speak in tongues.

We are told that tongues can build us up (just what every warrior needs.):

One who speaks in a tongue edifies himself; but one who prophesies edifies the church.

1 Corinthians 14:4

"Edify" means to build up. Some have missed what Paul was saying because of denominational prejudice. How can saying something you don't understand "build you up?" It's not because there is something intrinsically powerful about tongues, but rather that we're allowing the Holy Spirit to control our tongue. As we give our mind, our heart, our spirit over to the Lord, He fills us up, lifts us up, and builds us up. He, the Vine, pours His life-giving sap into us, the willing, drawing branch. The result is fruitfulness.

In 1 Corinthians 14, Paul is basically asking the believers to use restraint concerning speaking in tongues in a public meeting because it freaks some people out. He is seeking to limit speaking in tongues to times when someone will interpret the language so all can benefit (1 Corinthians 14:28). But, he quickly commands that no one forbid the speaking in tongues (verse 39), a point that many overlook.

Notice what he says in verse 18:

I thank God, I speak in tongues more than you all.

He speaks in tongues more than all of them. Why? Because he needed to be built up. After all, he spent most of his time ministering to others. Preachers, teachers and counselors can get into trouble if they are always pouring themselves out to others. Imagine how long a mother can nurse her infant if she's not eating anything. Praying in the Spirit fills us up, so that when others draw on us, we have something to give them. This is a spiritual exercise, and, therefore, of little direct value to our mind. Praise is a tool of the Holy Spirit for our mind, while tongues works mainly with our spirit.

When our mind gets into the habit of praising God for all things and in all things, and our spirit draws on the Holy Spirit through tongues, miraculous things happen.

Paul calls praying in tongues (verse 14), "praying in the spirit." The author of Jude uses this same phrase (verse 20) and tells us, as Paul does, that it builds us up. Ephesians 6:18 links praying in the Spirit (praying in tongues) to spiritual warfare. When you get exhausted in the daily battles of life, reach for refreshment – quickly turn on the power by praying in the Spirit and praising God freely. I believe this is what Paul had in mind in 2 Corinthians 6:7b

...by the weapons of righteousness for the right hand and the left hand!

In one hand we have the sword of our authority by which we bind the enemy forces; the other hand is raised in abandoned praise of our Awesome God who has all power.

Remember how I cautioned you to immediately put your focus back on the Lord after you bind a spirit and throw it into the abyss? The reason is that fighting drains us. Also, spirits are rebels, and they will pitch a fit until they absolutely have to go to the pit. As long as you stay focused on them and the problem they caused, they will loiter. Don't play their game; jump into the stream of God's Spirit and the splashing noise of the living water will drive them into the dark place. Your joyful praise will do almost as much as releasing your authority by binding and loosing.

*From the lips of children and infants you have ordained **praise** because of your enemies, to silence the foe and the avenger.*

Psalm 8:2 NIV

Praise is so powerful that children can use it to run the avenger off. Praise is our super weapon. Praise made the enemy run away from King Jehoshaphat (2 Chronicles 20:17-23), and it can blow your problems to smithereens. Philippians 4:6,7 tells us that prayer offered in thanksgiving releases the peace of God for our heart and our mind. It actually forms a fortress, a wall of the Holy Spirit around our mind and emotions (heart). If fighting wears you out, praise will build you up.

David praised God as he ran out to meet the huge giant (1 Samuel 17:45-47). Elijah praised God on Mount Carmel and brought down the fire of God to consume his sacrifice (1 Kings 18:36-38).

The opposite of praise, grumbling and complaining, leads to demonic bondage and death:

Nor grumble, as some of them did, and were destroyed by the destroyer.

1 Corinthians 10:10

Complaining is nothing other than agreeing with the enemy. The more we focus on his negative insight, the deeper we go into bondage (recall Romans 6:16 and 8:6). Instead, fight back with the devil-silencer – praise. Our goal needs to be to eradicate all complaining, negative insights, etc. and fill our minds with that which gives life.

Praise is faith in action. It is so powerful because it agrees with what the Word of God says. When we are instructed to praise God **for** all things and **in** all things, it is because God has promised to work **all things** together for our good. *If there is anything that you don't want God to turn into good for you, then don't thank Him for it.*

When we seek God for answers to serious problems, because they are heavy on our heart, we might have a tendency to pray with somber tones. We must be very careful because sad prayers can distract us, and turn our focus on the flesh instead of the Spirit.   Faith prayers, the kind that are full of the Holy Spirit, reach heaven and change things. Remember Romans 8:6.

Devote yourselves to prayer, keeping alert in it with an attitude of thanksgiving.

Colossians 4:2

We must learn to dwell in the Living Water, walk in the Spirit and flow in Love (Ephesians 3:14-21). When anything troubles the waters, we turn on the demonic intruder, send it packing, then rapidly refocus on our loving Father. If your day seems like it's starting out to be "one of those days," quickly pause for the refreshment of praise. Pray in tongues for a while, then switch over and praise with your mind. This is faith that works.

If you say you love the Lord and trust Him to meet your every need, then prove it by praising Him in advance!

If you agree with Jesus' words, *"for apart from Me you can do nothing"* (John 15:5), then don't get frustrated when things are out of your control; rather, praise Him for being in total control. Praise God when others let you down, not because they let you down, but because He's all you need, and He will never let you down. When others talk bad about you, praise God and don't try to set the record straight. As you throw yourself into the Living Water of the Holy Spirit through praise, He will do some "setting straight". He will fight for you; He will still the troublemaker.

People who have a hard time with teachings on praising God and with tongues may have been turned off by overzealous, unloving and insensitive people. So, who hasn't? But, people who resist these areas may have a faith problem. Some folks act like the Pentecostals have come up with weird doctrines, when in fact, the doubters are denying portions of the Scriptures. I say to them, quit fighting the Word of God and the Holy Spirit. Agree with His revealed will. Reach out for all the Lord has for you. Don't allow your faith to be built on the wisdom of man.

A great value with speaking in tongues is when pressure rises, and binding and loosing seems to fall on deaf ears (some demons play deaf). When I can't seem to pray with my mind, I can always pray in tongues. I turn my tongue over to the Holy Spirit and He takes it from there. Almost every time that binding doesn't work, praying in tongues breaks through the barrier. Why? Because it humbles the mind under the Holy Spirit. We are actually flowing with the Holy Spirit. We are agreeing with the Holy Spirit, and the agreement of two in prayer is promised to be effectual (Matthew 18:19).

Have an unsolvable mystery? Facing a dilemma? The enemy loves to drain our brain with trying to solve problems. The Word says that when we speak in tongues we speak mysteries (1 Corinthians 14:2). If we do as Paul suggests, and ask the Lord for the interpretation after we speak in tongues (verse 13), some of these mysteries will be revealed to us. Humble yourself under the Holy Spirit and pray in tongues until you sense a release. Ask in faith for the interpretation. Then, relax, knowing that the answer of the Spirit will soon arise in your understanding.

Remember our verse in Romans 8:6? How can I purposely put my mind on the Spirit and take it off the flesh, after all, we know how powerful the flesh is. Why not begin praising the Lord? In your mind see the Lord high and lifted up, sitting on His glorious throne. See yourself, bowing humbly, respectfully, at His feet. Softly, begin praying in the Spirit. Let your voice rise. Your prayer will be as incense to Him. Soon you will be praying in English, and you will feel the flow of the Holy Spirit. Give way to Him. Love Him. Praise this glorious God. Give over everything you can think of to Him. This is how the river begins to flow. Stay in the river.

The beauty of speaking in tongues is that you can do it any time, and not just out loud. Paul said that when no one was present who could interpret, "pray to yourself and to God" (1 Corinthians 14:28). Standing in line at a grocery store, pray in the spirit in your mind. When you are counseling someone, pray in the spirit. When you're being attacked verbally by someone, pray in the spirit. When pressures get too tough, get alone and pray in the spirit **out loud – loudly!**

This is powerful stuff. It breaks depression, anger, lust, sickness, etc., the whole time God gets the glory. No wonder the enemy tries so hard to steal this from believers.

If you've sought the baptism of the Holy Spirit with speaking in tongues and have not received, don't give up. There are many possible blockages.

As you patiently keep seeking, the Lord will show them to you. As you destroy each blockage by faith, you'll soon be free as a bird. Stinkin' thinkin' from the past can limit our faith, but you know what to do with Stinkin' Thinkin'.

If you've made fun of speaking in tongues, then an apology to the author of tongues is in order. This is what I had to do. If you're afraid of being embarrassed, or making a mistake, then you need to resist the spirit of fear and promptly submit to the Lord. If you've been taught against tongues by someone who refuses to accept the **whole** Bible, then you must choose who you're going to run with – this other person, or the God of the Bible. Jesus said we're to *"keep seeking, keep asking,"* so don't stop until you receive. If there's a blockage, it isn't on God's part, and your persistent faith will remove it.

Some say that gift of tongues is not for every believer, and I agree that the public gift of tongues is only for a few; however, the book of Acts evidence of being filled with the Holy Spirit is speaking in tongues (Acts 2:4; 10:46; 19:6). This is what Paul had and desired for all believers:

I thank God, I speak in tongues more than you all.

1 Corinthians 14:18

Now I wish that you all spoke in tongues, but even more that you would prophesy; and greater is one who prophesies than one who speaks in tongues, unless he interprets, so that the church may receive edifying.

1 Corinthians 14:5

Some folks misuse this verse to put down tongues, but it is clearly not a put-down, but a caution for public ministry. Paul was not impressed with the public gift of tongues, but he obviously used his private prayer language (verse 18, above) given by the Holy Spirit, very frequently.

THREE KEYS

I can't overemphasize three aspects of dealing with the Holy Spirit:

Stay needy; in need of Him. Declare Him to be your sufficiency. "Without you, I can do nothing."

Yield yourself totally to Him: your tongue, your hands, your past, your future, your job, your family, your whatever.

Develop a trusting friendship with the Holy Spirit through continual praise. Take His presence more serious than all the messy problems the enemy can throw at you.

Talk everything over with this One who was sent to keep us from feeling like orphans (John 14:18). He's called our Helper (John 14:16, 26), and will guide us into all truth (John 16:13). I like to sing the song, "Come Holy Spirit," as a fresh reminder that I need Him.

Often I ask Him, "Spirit of God, show me how to pray about_______." Develop a deep friendship with this One who was given to "walk alongside" (the meaning in the Greek). Get to know Him. Open up more and more to Him. Be filled and refilled. Not just for your own enjoyment, but as a paramedic, traveling the streets of life, always ready to dispense the healing balm to hurting people.

The early church was visited mightily on the Day of Pentecost. They were endued with great power. But soon the devil had the religious people so whipped up with jealous stinkin' thinkin' that they arrested the new believers. After the muckety-mucks threatened the "spiritually high" saints, the believers returned to their meeting place, rather drained. They went into some serious prayer, and the Holy Spirit was poured out on them again, and they were filled afresh. New power. That's why the Word says:

...be continually filled with the Holy Spirit.

Ephesians 5:18 (from the Greek)

SNARE WATCH

Watch for these snares:

- When we fuss with each other, the Spirit pulls back.

- Pride that we do or don't speak in tongues.

- Feeling that a situation justifies you taking control without asking the Lord.

- Saying, "Oh well, I couldn't help it; I'm just a weak human," instead of seeking God's power.

Failure is not so much a matter of me not being able to live the Christian life; it's a matter of my pride. Will I admit I can't do it without the Holy Spirit and surrender totally to Him for His powerful infilling, or will I quit because I can't be perfect, and refuse to do anything – which is ultimate pride.

It's as simple as staying needy; as easy as yielding everything to Him; declaring His way is best even when we can't understand how or why, by praising Him in advance.

Chapter 11

NEW RUTS FOR OLD

If you've faithfully tried the steps out-lined so far and still feel like a failure, consider the force of ruts. If the power of the Holy Spirit still seems beyond your reach, even though you have sincerely sought for it, suspect the subtlety of ruts. You are probably coming to a showdown with "Habit Patterns," one of the meanest hombres in the West.

Remember when we looked at Romans 7:20? Paul stated that because he did not want to do what he was doing, it wasn't him doing it. This wasn't double-talk. It's true. When we do what we don't want to do, then something else is exerting pressure upon us – at first. As Ephesians 6:12 explains, the origin of our troubles is from the foe. But, here's the subterfuge:

Once we've developed a habit pattern in our life by repeated obedience of the enemy, we are his servant.

Do you not know that when you present yourselves to someone as slaves for obedience, you are slaves of the one whom you obey, either of sin resulting in death, or of obedience resulting in righteousness?

Romans 6:16

We can fool ourselves into thinking we're basically an innocent victim, but repeated failure digs a rut. The mind's ability to perform a function without conscious effort is tapped by our adversary and used against us. This ability is good when it comes to driving cars and doing a host of other routine jobs. It's a dangerously different matter when our "routine" skills include complaining, doubting, lusting, drinking, fighting, lying, etc.

Binding and loosing may not yield much success if the instigator is long gone, and **we** are the culprit. When a habit is formed by obeying the enemy's repetitive suggestions, the tempter is no longer required. Who is at fault? We are. Where did the temptation come from? Initially, Satan, but our continued obedience produces a bondage, slavery. Who gets into trouble? We do. How do we break the bondage, chase away the enemy? It's probably too late for that. No, we must do something with the rut.

RUTS

We know that ruts are formed in dirt roads by constant traffic. Even asphalt streets get ruts when used excessively. In our lives, we tend to repeat old patterns, ***especially if they seem to work.*** Before very long we have a habit that we can do without consciously thinking. This capacity of the mind is great if we're running certain machinery, but it's a killer when we're dealing with stinkin' thinkin'. If it's "second nature" for us to doubt, fear, cuss, hit, etc., the enemy can use this otherwise productive aspect of our mind to destroy us.

Ruts have great power over us because they become our **reflex** or first response. We do them without stopping to think, and, therefore, our enemy has only to flash a picture across our mind, and we take it from there. If the rut was encouraged by an evil spirit, then the spirit becomes a source of pressure that keeps us in the rut. The spirit may have an easy job, and only stirs when we try to shake ourselves free.

We know that demons can't trap us unless they trick us into using our will against ourselves. I don't believe they can snare us by just an occasional oversight on our part. However, when we have obeyed their impulses and temptations over a period of time, we find ourselves in a rut with the evil spirit as our taskmaster. We may want to get out of the rut, but find it virtually impossible. We may go forward for prayer in special meetings and find some relief for a season, but soon the old rut returns.

I believe there are four very important things we must do to get out and stay out of deadly ruts:

1. SAY "STOP"

At the first sign of stinkin' thinkin' you have a choice. This is when it will be the easiest to change directions. An old adage is that it's harder to gather the chickens after they get loose. So, when you first notice the rut response starting, say loudly in your mind, "**STOP!**"

When you come to a fork in the road at full speed, you'll end up going the way you have always gone. You need to come to a complete stop and **think!** When you first feel yourself getting angry, say "**STOP**" in your mind. When old depression thoughts start to roll in, just say "**STOP!**"

2. MAKE A CHOICE!

You do not have to continue living the same old way. How could God hold us responsible for changing if we "can't help it"? We can choose a different response. God puts before us life and death and asks us to make the choice for life (Deuteronomy 30: 19,20). But:

The biggest problem with ruts is that you can do the wrong thing without even thinking!

See the end result of the wrong action. See the benefits of doing what is right, what you really want to do. **Then make your decision for the new**

way, the best way, the way of life. Say this decision to yourself over and over until the power of repetition begins to create a habit.

As an example, let's say your rut of stinkin' thinkin' has to do with feeling like a failure and that things are never going to get any better. When you sense the failure feelings starting to rise, say **stop**, then picture where the path of failure thinking will take you... right to a junk pile. Picture yourself walking down the path of LIFE with Jesus, hand in hand. Choose the path of Life. Say over and over, "Jesus, I choose to walk the Path of Life with You. You are leading me in success and abundance. Things are getting better and better."

Memorize a couple of verses like Psalm 35:27 or Psalm 36:7-9. Say them over and over to yourself.   Instead of allowing the enemy to use the power of repetition to beat you down, use it to create Life –

ABUNDANT LIFE!

You will probably have to say your positive response out loud as well as in your mind. I'm convinced that the recordings that go over and over in our mind are where the greatest power exists. So, get new recordings. The deeper the rut, the more work it will take to make a new one; but, whatever the effort required, it will be worth it.

One person told me how effective it was for them to jump in their car and go for a ride and yell at the top of their lungs at the devil. They were intensifying this principle of making a choice. When they yelled, they were convincing themselves as well as the enemy. The bottom line was that it broke the enemy's grip. I say, Hallelujah, whatever it takes. Let's win.

3. SEND SOMEBODY TO JAIL!

We discussed this in detail in chapters two and three. Resist the force that is trying to keep you in the rut. Put a name on it. What is the rut? Set the name of the rut up as a target, and shoot at it with your weaponry. Use the name of Jesus to bind it and then send it packing to the abyss.

"Rut (or spirit) of negative thinking, I demand you leave me right now in the name of Jesus."

Or . . .

"Spirit of lust I bind you in Jesus' name. You will not lure me into your filth."

Lock up the critters in the abyss. The main point is that we will need to get the "unseen" pressure off our back if we are to win the scrimmage. The enemy pounds hard against our mind to trick us into using our will for his ends. Don't fall for it. **Resist the pressure to sin as though it were from a deadly fortress – it is.**

4. DO SOMETHING NEW

New, Spirit-given ruts are what we want. Wouldn't it be great if it was second nature for you to have loving, faith responses to problems instead of blowing up? It can happen, but it will require making new habits. What I'm trying to say with step four is that we can't merely stop doing negative things. We must start doing new, positive things or we'll slip back into the old ruts.

How about an example of using these four steps? Let's say you feel a wave of depression coming over you. **First**, say **STOP. Secondly**, see in your mind a negative picture of the probable consequences from acting on the depression. Contrast that picture with one of you being successful in repulsing the temptation. Make the decision to not accept the negative rut. Speak your decision out loud. **Thirdly**, bind the spirit that put the pressure on you (thoughts and emotions), and send him packing. **Fourthly**, begin praising God for the victory, the new life, the abundance He's giving you. Put some positive faith responses to work in your mind. This is when it's valuable to have some memory verse cards close by. Pull one out and focus on what God has said.

If the rut-pressure is to think something judgmental toward someone, then a good, new response would be to bless them instead.

THE PRICE

Victory has a price. It would be nice if we could have someone say a little prayer for us and then be on our way and never have to fight the devil again. But, alas, it doesn't work that way. That would be heaven. This is the schoolroom called life, and it comes fully equipped with exciting tests and opportunities for growth.

You may drive into a ditch that is too close to the road, and a tow truck can pull you out. If, however, something isn't done with the ditch and your driving doesn't improve, you'll probably soon be back in the ditch. We must learn how to drive in the Spirit to avoid the ditches, and then pay the price to get the ditches filled up.

The Bible is full of instructions on how to "drive" properly, such as "flee youthful lusts," "don't let the sun go down on your wrath," etc. As you are reading along in the Word, some of these might jump out at you. If they do, don't argue with the Lord, telling Him how that's not a problem with you. Who do you think made it jump out at you? Prayerfully consider such verses, and whisper a prayer like, "Lord Jesus, show me how to incorporate this truth in my life to a greater degree."

When I took Judo as a teenager, our teacher drilled us for months on how to fall properly. In Judo, especially when you're first learning, you spend a lot of time flying through the air and landing in a pile. The teacher's goal was for us to automatically land in such a way that we would minimize getting hurt. After months of slapping the mats, I knew how to land – automatically.

The price I paid to learn how to take a fall paid big dividends. Not only did I escape injury during two years of Judo, but one day it saved my back. I fell from a rafter when I was goofing off at camp – straight down on my back, on a wood floor. Without even thinking, I slapped the floor as though it were a Judo mat. I broke the fall and, I believe, saved my back from serious injury. The moral to this story: **When you pay a price to discipline yourself for godliness, you will automatically do the right thing at the right time!** And it can save more than your physical body.

RUT DETECTORS

How can we tell if we are in serious ruts? It may not be as obvious as you think to determine if you have been tricked by an enemy spirit into a destructive habit pattern. Some of these ruts hide behind family traits, nationality quirks and survival devices. For instance, you've heard people blame their hot temper on their Irish lineage or their red hair or that they were just like their father. What they're saying is that they can't be expected to change, after all, it's not their fault. If you find yourself doing something your parents used to do that drove you crazy, you probably adopted one of their ruts without even realizing it.

RESPONSIBILITY

We are responsible for our own actions and reactions. Sometimes we might be heard to say, "Well, that's just my personality. That's just the way I am." We don't get out of ruts by blaming someone else or excusing away our shortcomings. **Growth is a personal response.** People can nag us to change, and we can wish that change would come, but lasting growth is only possible when we make a firm resolve to change and then take whatever steps are necessary to walk out the change.

How does the enemy figure into breaking habit patterns? Picture a man trying to climb out of a ditch, but he has a heavy pack on his back. You say to him, "Hey, why don't you climb out of the ditch?" He answers, "I really want to, but I have this heavy pack on my back and I don't have the strength to get out." We may think he is silly for not casting the pack off his back and scampering out of the ditch, but he has come to believe that the pack is a necessity for his life. Spirits work like the pack on the back. They can convince us that they are absolutely essential for our life.

Behind the ruts and behind the spirits there is the truth of the first few chapters. Bad behavior starts in the mind. You may not agree with this next statement, but I feel that even habits such as smoking are not as much a physical addiction to nicotine as they are a destructive rut in the thinking processes.

When someone makes up their mind to quit smoking, a battle starts. It's not a physical battle as much as it is the mind being bombarded by thoughts from the spirit behind the rut of smoking. Sure, chemical reactions can cause discomfort for a while as the physical body adapts to the absence of nicotine, but this passes in a short time. For a long-term smoker, the battle lasts much longer than the chemical readjustment. There's something more going on.

A little voice says, "Man, wouldn't a smoke go good right now?" Your mind (thinking it was your own thought) answers back, "Yes, but I just quit." If there were no pressure from outside sources at this point, you would change the subject and be on about your business. But there is a spirit behind the rut of smoking – Mr. Nicotine.

A royal battle ensues. The spirit tells you that you need something to calm your nerves. It says you are going to eat yourself to death if you don't start smoking again, etc. And, the worst part of all, the little imp reminds you how great it was to have a cigarette and a cup of coffee. These stinkers seem to know just what memory to recall to try to talk us back into the rut.

If the habit breaker is ignorant of what we talked about in the preceding chapters, he's going to have a rough time walking in victory. But, if the person sees what's going on and fights the spiritual battle and then fills up the rut with new actions, victory is near. I've talked to many people who won the fight for freedom from binding habits, and the way they know the victory is complete is when there's not the slightest tug toward the old response. This takes determined effort, but it's worth it.

I used smoking as an example because many of us have fought furiously to quit smoking, or know someone who has, only to lose the battle. I believe that something like this scenario is working behind every destructive habit, from cussing to pornography to temper flare-ups to charge-mania to phobias and depression.

TRAPDOORS

Ruts started somewhere, and if we can determine when and how they started, we are more liable to keep from falling back into the trap or into a parallel trap. Ruts don't "just happen." For something like smoking, a poke into the past may reveal a teenager who was determined to be liked by the crowd and thus began the "in" habit. Maybe it was a desire to be macho or cool. If the acquisition of the habit was to spite someone, then a spirit of rebellion might be connected with keeping us in the rut.

Someone told me that he would have quit smoking sooner if people hadn't bugged him about quitting – sounds like a spirit of pride was involved.

Another trapdoor can be overeating because of being raised in poverty. A panic spirit subconsciously suggests that we'd better eat every-thing in sight because this may be the last of the food, or our brother might get it first.

I know that some women were harassed or abused when they were slim and trim, so they decided to protect themselves inside large castle walls. These self-protective thoughts make a bit of sense, but they are a replacement for dependence upon the Living God. They are actually an idol, a substitute for the faith that the Lord will supply our needs, fight for us, etc.

Ask the Holy Spirit, "Where did this rut begin?" And then seek His guidance if there might be some alien mischief-makers helping you to stay in the rut. You probably won't hear an audible voice, but He will more than likely, within a few days, bring to your mind where it all began.

The trapdoor for depression is usually tied into losing hope. We want to have a handle on life, yet we feel helplessly out of control. We can get into the rut of listening to a spirit of depression sing a woeful tale of how bad things are, how misunderstood we are, or that the future is hopeless.

A controlling spirit tries to get us to control as much of life as we can. When we can't control our circumstances or the people around us, we can slip into depression or anger. Depression is not always caused by these things. Sometimes it is caused by hormone imbalance (monthly cycles, etc.) or other physical problems; however, by far, most depression ruts are from stinkin' thinkin'.If you were the tempter and wanted to get people to try to control others, what kinds of thoughts would you stick in their heads?

There is no way we can discuss all the trap doors that lead to ruts. But, you're   intelligent enough to find the trapdoors that need correcting. Besides, you have the Holy Spirit, Who, by the way, is more concerned about this than you are. Seek His guidance.

Monitor your thinking patterns for a while. Look for thoughts with a false promise. A spirit of lying promises to get us out of trouble and supply whatever we need. The power behind a macho image likewise promises great things but never comes through. A spirit of failure may promise the perfect excuse – "You can't expect me to succeed."

The spirit that suggests we throw a temper tantrum gives the idea that acting crazy provides power. This can be carried over into adulthood and produce a monster. These ruts of unsuitable behaviors resulted from continual repetition of wrong actions because we somehow saw the benefits as greater than any consequences. We may have thought to ourselves, "I really shouldn't act this way, but so what, it works, doesn't it?"

If an adult has a rut of throwing temper tantrums that are a carryover from childhood, the only lasting solution must start with a surrender of one's whole life to the Lordship of Jesus. A new thinking rut needs to be implemented:

"Jesus, I don't want things to go my way; please let them go Your way!"

This kind of phrase, running through your mind, develops a new rut, one with unlimited power. The temper tantrum response is selfish; this new rut of turning control of your life over to Jesus by an act of your will is selfless. One produces life, the other produces death.

Sometimes a friend can help us determine how we got into a particular rut and what the power is behind the rut. Other people can usually be more objective about our problems than we can. Be careful who you choose to talk to if you are dealing with a sensitive or embarrassing area. Not everyone can keep things quiet.

Try to think back to when you first noticed the problem becoming a pattern. If you find the start of a rut, you'll probably find something that you need to confess and repent of before the Lord.

As an example, let's say you trace a rut of fear back to a time when you were scared as a child. You were walking home in the dark and your bully brother jumped out of the bushes and scared you silly. In the moments following the incident, as you collected your senses, anger probably arose, and blended in with the fear. As similar events occurred, a spirit of fear started helping you out by warning you in advance of when and where you might get scared by bully brother or perhaps something even more dangerous. It made sense to consider the advance warnings, after all, it's better to be scared only a little bit rather than the mega dose you first experienced.

Somewhere along life's path, "Fear, the helper" turned into "Fear, a taskmaster," a rut in which you are trapped. The Scriptural way to prevent such a rut from developing in the first place is to take every situation captive to Christ. You would have had to forgive your mean brother and then reaffirm that the Lord is your constant Shepherd and friend and that He would always protect you. Such a biblical response to a scary experience prevents a spirit from taking advantage of your vulnerability. Then, filling your mind with positive thoughts, such as are found in the Bible, makes the perfect rut fill-er-upper.

There may not be a spirit behind the negative ruts in our lives, but because Ephesians 6:12 specifically tells us that we are not wrestling against flesh and blood, the truth is that the enemy is probably involved to one degree or another. Our opponent, according to God, is extraterrestrial – demonic powers of the dark spheres. Fight the wrong enemy and you get nowhere; fight the right enemy and you win. Beating on our self sometimes seems to make sense, but if we're not the main culprit – we get no where.

Chapter 12

HINDRANCES TO WINNING

The other day a parent told me that they started to scold their child for fighting with their sister, when the child said, "It wasn't my fault; the devil made me do it." The youngster was able to pinpoint the source of the trouble, but guess who got the spanking. One of the hardest things to sort out in our minds is the difference between where our responsibility starts and where the devil's mischief ends. If we miss the difference, we're the one who ends up getting the spanking by life.

Have you been tempted to put some of your responsibility off on the devil, when **you** were the one who played too long with the enemy's bait? [no need to raise your hand]

MAJOR HINDRANCES TO WINNING

1. RECOGNIZING THE   SOURCE OF CONFLICT

It's good for us to periodically be reminded that the sinister foe of our soul still has to work with our will. He can bluff, use subterfuge, roar, etc., but the bottom line is, we have to fall for his weed-seed. Stinkin' thinkin' may start with input from the pit, but if we entertain it, we're the ones who will have to pay the bill. Our enemy is limited to working by the same laws of faith that the entire Kingdom of God uses.

Where do we draw the line between when junk is from us and when it's from our rival? This is a review question. Go back through the series and relocate the seven signs when it's not you thinking stinky. Review is good.

We need to make a big deal out of this issue until it becomes a habit, a good rut of sorting out negative input. This is true holiness. This is sanctification made simple. If we keep our inner sanctuary clean and pure out of love for our Lord, it is a very high form of worship. Such a lifestyle is power-producing, joy-releasing, and Father pleasing.

Simply put, if we depend on the Scriptures and the Holy Spirit, we will be able to divide between when thoughts are ours and when they are an opportunity to lock up some foul spirit.

For the word of God is living and active and sharper than any two-edged sword, and piercing as far as the division of soul and spirit, of both joints and marrow, and able to judge the thoughts and intentions of the heart.

Hebrews 4:12

Let's say you're pondering Colossians 2:8-10 in your devotions:

See to it that no one takes you captive through philosophy and empty deception, according to the tradition of men, according to the elementary principles of the world, rather than according to Christ. For in Him all the fullness of Deity dwells in bodily form, and in Him you have been made complete, and He is the head over all rule and authority.

...and suddenly, seemingly out of nowhere, a feeling of worthlessness sweeps over you. The words of a significant adult from your past comes to you with a piercing, haunting sensation – "You'll never amount to anything." Was that you? Maybe you just have a bad self-image. But, what does the Word of God say?

Don't be confused. Worldly psychology is not aware that we have a real, unseen enemy. They say we're the problem; the Bible says that Satan and his demons are the problem.

Who comes immediately to steal the Word of God away from us? [see Mark 4:15]   How can we know the truth if he's always standing by, snatching it away? Remember, praise the Lord, the enemy has to depend upon us believing his fleshly evidence rather than accepting God's **facts.** If you read that you are complete in Jesus and the liar says you're a mess, go with God's evidence.

Any input that belittles, that discourages, that confines to failure, is from the enemy.

2.   DOUBLE-MINDED

But let him ask in faith without any doubting, for the one who doubts is like the surf of the sea driven and tossed by the wind. For let not that man expect that he will receive anything from the Lord, being a double-minded man, unstable in all his ways.   James 1:6-8

If having a double-mind will keep the power of God from flowing in our life, then we should expect the enemy to try to get us to ponder **tug-of-war** thoughts. One minute we are strong in faith, claiming that the Word is true; the next minute we're tempted to bow down at the altar of feelings – feelings that contradict the Word. We can actually feel like we're going crazy, when all that is taking place is harassment. Harassed by emotions.

Could I get you to do a little faith exercise? Would you say this statement to yourself, right now:

Feelings are not the Lord over my life, Jesus is. I do not owe my feelings anything. I purpose to set my mind on the things of the Holy Spirit, that I might enjoy peace and life.

The reason I wanted you to say this is that the longer I talk to people, the more I see the enemy's most clever device is to throw feelings at us. Most folks are thrown off balance when temptations come as feelings. Our spirit knows better, but our mind grabs onto the feelings. Suddenly we're double-minded.

Can you see why the enemy goes for making us double-minded? Once we get suspicious of feelings that are negative or that are contrary to God's promises, it's a snap for us to win. Our adversary depends on our being ignorant of his tricks. Once we see how we've literally worshiped our feelings, we're on our way out of the failure rut.

HOW'S YOUR LOVE LIFE?

Double-mindedness gets dangerous when we have a strong desire to follow the Lord, but we can't seem to let go of the old habits that once bound us. Something inside us says we still love the old ways, yet we know we want to serve the Lord. The emotions that say we love the old, sinful ways, are lying. Do you remember Romans 7:20? The Apostle Paul struggled with this same emotional tug-of-war. His Spirit-given conclusion was: If I don't want to sin, the pressure to sin must be from somewhere else. Don't be fooled if temptation comes masquerading as a "love" for some old sin. If my spirit person doesn't want it, then it's not me; it's sin.

Our feelings will vary depending upon what we are thinking about. If you think of something sad, you'll soon feel sad. If you think of something funny, you'll find your face slipping into a grin. As we watch TV, our feelings can bounce back and forth as we observe different things. **Our focus dictates our feelings.** And what is even crazier, the sad scene in a movie is phoney; it's a set. If we saw the actual event as it was being filmed, we would have a far different emotional response.

God's Word gives us a purer, higher picture. From the perspective of His promises we can see where the negative emotions are coming from and objectively choose to deny them.

We do not owe our feelings anything !

GANGING UP

Add to this confusion, friends that are still in the old paths. They will have a hard time understanding our new desires. If pleasing them is a high priority, we will be tempted to have two masters and thus be double-minded. Have you felt this confusion, wanting to please the Lord, but wanting to please your old friends? How have you handled it, or have you?

I hear people say that it's hard to live the Christian life. What I think they are trying to sort through are these feelings of the new love versus the old loves.

If it seems hard to win the inner war, check to see if you still have a fond place in your heart for old, sinful activities. Do you cherish some memories that, when honest, you must admit are not pleasing to the Lord?

Some of your rowdy times from the past may include what David described in the Psalms as "sins of my youth." In that which is clearly offensive to us now, may lurk an event that gives us warm fuzzy feelings as we reflect upon it. If all sin is not gross to us, then we are aiding and abetting the enemy. As was said of the kings of old:

And Jehoash did right in the sight of the Lord all his days in which Jehoiada the priest instructed him. Only the high places were not taken away; the people still sacrificed and burned incense on the high places.   2 Kings 12:2,3

Frequently in the book of 2 Kings, revival is described as coming short of being complete with the above phrase, "Only the high places were not taken away." Incomplete cleansing of the old ways laid the groundwork for shallow revival. We want complete victory and total joy, but unless we completely eradicate the old habits, we'll be unable to enjoy all that we desire. We must cultivate a new appetite for godliness and a new hatred of sin, even warm fuzzy sin.

What James 1:6-8 is saying is that we may not have to actually sell out to sin to get into trouble. Vacillating back and forth between wanting to please the Lord and desiring to do our own thing will prevent our victory. I have a tendency to think that if a person really wants God's best, then everything is OK. The bigger picture is that if they still love sin, their desires for God are as powerful as hoping to win the lottery. If the enemy can trick us into thinking that we still love sin, he can whip on us and our prayer guns are shut down.

"Trick us into thinking we still love sin? Don't you have that wrong?"

No, the born-again part of us, the spirit, loves God and hates sin. If our mind agrees with our spirit, we'll be single-minded. If our mind agrees with the flesh (sin, the enemy), our spirit will still hate sin, but then we'll be double-minded. Our mind can either love sin or hate it. Our spirit, however, can only hate sin.

Let me try an example. Let's say Borris is trying to stop being a nag. For years he's come home from work and started picking on Matilda, his lovely wife. Then he starts in on the kids. They can't do anything right. Pick-pick, nag-nag. Everybody's sick of it and they threaten to walk out. In desperation, Borris contacts Pastor Wiffle. The pastor breaks the bad news to Borris – stinkin' thinkin'. The cure: you cannot entertain the negative "insights" about others that the enemy throws into your mind, and not have them come slithering out your mouth.

When Borris sees the negative "insights" about his family members in light of the Word of God, he will begin to hate the thoughts. As long as he sees the negative put-downs as "cool" or "right," the family will suffer if they are around him. Borris must develop a hatred for every thought that does not convey mercy, grace, hope, and love.

DOUBLE-MINDED GLITTER

Believing the false claims of sin is another way we can be double-minded. The enemy has been doing a con job on us humans for the past 6,000 years, that the Kingdom of God is inferior to the wealth, glitter, lusts, and sensations of this world. God gave us this world to enjoy; our enemy wants us to worship it – exalt it above its Creator.

God gave us sex as a beautiful picture and expression of interacting, covenant love. Satan pushes some people into worshiping sex and thereby actually become bound by it. Women have been known to starve themselves to death in order to be "sexy." Some will chance deadly disease in order to have sex.

Many have been brain-damaged by the Perverter's lies: the worldly "twist" is better than the "straight life" God expects us to live. This lie must be totally dug out of our minds if we are to eliminate double-mindedness. It only took a short time to get the children of Israel out of Egypt, but it took forty years to get Egypt out of them. Even then, some of the old-timers died rather than let go of the philosophies of Egypt. Our entire life is an exercise in becoming whole: becoming single-minded in our values, in our desires, in our evaluation of what constitutes quality. Success comes from agreeing with our born-again spirit, the Word of God, and the Holy Spirit.

To become single-minded in this way is not as hard as you might think.

Just cut the debates, drop the comparisons, and refuse to consider the enemy's devaluation of God's Word!

If Eve had done this in the Garden, wow, we'd all be in heaven. Satan says, "Aw, God doesn't want you to eat that fruit because He's afraid that it'll make you as smart as Him." Suppose Eve had said, "*I'm not going to debate God's Word. **Get lost.**"* That's about as hard as it's supposed to be to win over the enemy.

Instead, she looked at the forbidden fruit. She rubbed on it. She pondered how it would make her feel. It was hard to resist temptation only because she was playing with incomplete, false evidence that was contradictory to God's Word. Like our first mother, we may fiddle around with sin and its claims and then whimper about how hard it is to resist sin. Not too smart.

Imagine how stunted an education we'd have if we didn't debate the excitement of sin and the boredom of God's promises. Why, we might never know the thrill of sickness, disease, death, sweat from toil, birth pains, etc. All those great fruits from the fall of mankind would be missed. Now that would be a shame, wouldn't it?

When we play with the devil's false "facts" as though we owe it to ourselves to be informed on both sides of the issues of life, we are on our way to becoming double-minded.

Once double-minded, we have no prayer power and thus we're a sitting duck for the roaring lion (does he eat ducks?).

DOUBLE-MINDED MERCY

Consider double-mindedness from another angle. If I want to flow in mercy and grace, yet hold unforgiveness toward anyone, then I am trying to mix death and life. I am, in effect, of two opinions. I'm trying to serve two masters. My spiritual authority over the devil is put on the shelf when I give him an opportunity by obeying his temptations. Yes, I have a new problem when I'm nursing a grudge. If I receive a bad report on anyone, then the Holy Spirit must back off. The Comforter hangs around with mercy and grace, but He gets offended when people accuse others.

STUBBORN SPIRITS

Suppose that I detect an accusing spirit operating on my mind. I immediately bind the spirit that supplied the accusing thought and cast it into the abyss. But, what if I do not have the assurance it left because I can still feel the pressure to make someone "shape up," and I hear its offensive badgering. Why won't it go? Don't I have authority over it?

We should have authority over all evil spirits, but if one refuses to leave, then begin to suspect that you gave the critter an open door of opportunity (Ephesians 4:27). When we receive devil-data (weed-seed), and ponder on it, we become subservient to our enemy.

Remember Romans 6:16?

Do you not know that when you present yourselves to someone as slaves for obedience, you are slaves of the one whom you obey, either of sin resulting in death, or of obedience resulting in righteousness?

We actually give our enemy the advantage over us when we, mercy-bought believers, allow anger producing thoughts to remain in our mind. As they fester, they'll foul up our whole life. Anger and grudges are mental responses designed to get us to side with the "Accuser of the Brethren" (Revelation 12:10). How double- minded can you get?

SMALL SNARES

Jesus said that we will be faithful in big things if we are faithful in small things. This being so, our enemy only needs to get us to mess around with small sins. Something as simple as being double-minded is all it takes to quench the Spirit and start cooling down the fires of revival and activate the power of death.

Here's some of the small things that the enemy will try to catch us on:

JUDGING SOMEONE'S MOTIVES:

Most would be quick to say they are not God, but when they judge as though they know someone's motives, the secrets of their heart, they are trying to take over God's job. This can be a small thing that becomes a big problem. It produces pride and pride results in God resisting the judge. To some degree most of us fight this, so what kind of faith-seed (self-talk) can you suggest for the person fighting judgmental thoughts? It would be excellent to have some verses memorized that we could say to ourselves in place of judgmental thoughts.

BAD NEWS:

We know God is going to provide for all those who love Him, yet if we allow a sick feeling to remain for a while after we hear bad news, it's a little thing that can become a big problem. The author of   negative feelings needs to be locked up. Do you think it's OK to have a "sick" feeling when you hear bad news? How big of a deal is this? Where can it lead?

BEING LET DOWN:

We know no one is perfect, yet if we freak out when someone lets us down for the Nth time, it's a little thing that can become a big problem. Worse yet, if we explode, like that's going to change them, we'll make matters worse. We need to explode at the one dredging up the negative evidence. What kind of stinkin' thinkin' does the enemy use to make matters worse when people let us down?

VALID DISCERNMENT

When the Accuser of the brethren tricks us into acting upon a non-grace thought, we are swindled into relinquishing some of our authority. This is why the Word warns us against receiving accusations unless there are several witnesses (1 Timothy 5:19). The adversary loves to lure us away from mercy.

"But what if someone is in gross sin? Aren't we supposed to do something?"

We were instructed to take every thought captive to Jesus in 2 Corinthians 10:5. When there seems to be sufficient warrant for our consideration, such as someone purposefully hurting others, lay all the evidence at the feet of Jesus. Ask Him what He would have you do with this data. He may ask you to approach leadership with the information or merely pray over it, seeking grace for the offender. Don't ponder on the data by yourself lest you play host to the accuser of the brethren. **Flowing in grace does not mean we're to ignore sin; it does mean we're to seek God for the best response.**

When in doubt, talk to someone who is sensitive to spiritual things. My main concern is that when we see people around us walking in sin, we might simmer inside, or gossip about them to others. To avoid being double-minded with mercy or side-tracked with judging, seek the Lord for discernment. His Word can show us what to do in any situation.

MURPHY'S LAW

You've heard of Murphy's Law, haven't you? *"If anything can go wrong, it will."* There are many axioms related to this storehouse of negative nonsense. One of these can wiggle its way inside our mind and sidetrack our faith. Our Spirit-controlled mind becomes confused with foolish speculations. We get paranoid, looking over our shoulder, expecting bad things to happen. *"Oh, oh, things have been going too smoothly, something freaky is probably going to happen soon."* Our society is full of this crazy foolishness and it is totally opposite of what God wants our minds to be focusing on. If we let this junk slosh around in our brain, the end result will be double-mindedness.

3. SUNDAY SAINTS

Let's look at one more big hindrance to winning the inner war. If we have two compartments to our life, a church side and a world side, we'll have a hard time experiencing anywhere near the joy and happiness that Jesus designed for us to enjoy. "Hypocrite" is a word that is often used to describe people that have one lifestyle on Sundays at church and another on Monday morning at work. But, let me say something that you may think is absolutely dumb. Some folks may not know that they don't have to be living two different lifestyles.

If they are truly born-again, then they are a new creature. Their spirit person wants to be just like Jesus all the time. Their mind may simply be believing the lies of the enemy that they need the favor or acceptance of the world. Talking with Jesus throughout the day will make Him a real part of their life. Soon He will begin to shine through them to people at work, home, school, etc.

Some folks may live two different lives because that's all they've seen. Maybe they were raised by God-fearing parents that had double standards – one for church, and another for everywhere else. Just because they get excited about the Lord doesn't mean they will automatically know how to live a single-minded lifestyle.

How much of a Christian witness does God expect of us when we're away from church? Are leaders the only ones expected to live differently? What about ordinary believers? Consider the story Jesus told of three guys that were given talents (a measure of money in Bible days). The fellow who was given the least amount, buried his talent, maybe out of spite. What I want us to reflect on is that he did not take his assignment seriously. Notice what Jesus said about this man:

And cast out the worthless slave into the outer darkness; in that place there shall be weeping and gnashing of teeth.

Matthew 25:30

We have a commission from the Master. He made us, and, He fully expects us to be a 24-hour example of His love. We're not here to do our own thing, stick up for our little reputation, be entertained all the time. We're to abide in Him like the branch on a grapevine, drawing in all His love and grace. The natural byproduct will be fruit that others will be blessed by. If we bury our Christianity to keep from being hassled by others, how will they ever see the fruit that leads to eternal life?

Maybe the wicked servant hid his talent because he was afraid of making mistakes. Perhaps stinkin' thinkin' from his childhood taunted him—*"you'll never amount to anything...   you always mess up every-thing."* We know what to do with those kinds of thoughts, right?

THE CLEANSING

Draw near to God and He will draw near to you. Cleanse your hands, you sinners; and purify your hearts, you double-minded.

James 4:8

Isn't this verse saying that double-mindedness is a purity problem? Double-mindedness must mean that there is something in the heart that doesn't belong there. Repentance is the reset button our mind can push to wash away clutter and pollution. Confessing sin and receiving God's fresh application of grace and mercy causes the house to be cleansed. But for us to be able to push this button of repentance, we must be sick of the sin. Do we really hate this thing that came between us and our Awesome God? Is the absence of His grace a greater pain than the shallow pleasure of being right, harboring bitterness, or playing with sin? When we're repulsed by sin, its power to pollute our heart begins to wane.

We will only be in this physical existence for a little while. What we do while we're here can help a bunch of people find eternal life, or we can selfishly try to store up supplies on a sinking ship. In a short time, habits will no longer be important, hobbies will pass away, and body beautiful will return to dust. Relaxing and enjoying life will take a sudden turn. If we've missed the main point of the Bible and have taken life too seriously, we'll be eternally regretful.

If, instead, we step back from all the commotion and pressure to be an external person, and seek the Author of Life inside, in our sanctuary, we'll be eternally blessed. In the in-between time, the godliness we develop will be profitable for both now and later (1 Timothy 4:8). Godliness will release the anointing, which will in turn, protect, heal, witness, meet needs, fulfill, enrich, and make our life overflow with love. This is the ultimate perspective. This is a war well won.

REFLECTIONS

Has this study helped you? It can be a great benefit if you write some of these things out and review them once a week for a month or so. The Word says, "As iron sharpens iron, so one man sharpens another." If this study has helped, now sharpen someone else.

Appendix A

WHAT DOES IT MEAN TO BE A CHRISTIAN

The Bible tells us how we can enjoy a rich, fulfilling life. The Awesome Creator designed us with a capacity for love and a desire to be successful. This abundant life was formulated around mankind living in close fellowship with the Lord. Listen to the words of Jesus Christ:

Here I am! I stand at the door and knock. If anyone hears My voice and opens the door, I will come in and eat with him, and he with Me.

Revelation 3:20

God's design includes provisions for us even when we're physically and emotionally drained:

Come to Me, all you who are weary and burdened, and I will give you rest.

Matthew 11:28

Yes, our loving Father God has our best in mind:

...I have come that they may have life, and have it to the full.

John 10:10b

I have told you this so that My joy may be in you and that your joy may be complete.

John 15:11

Why is it that most people are not experiencing this abundance? Mankind has stepped out of God's plan and has tried to do their own thing. The Bible calls this sin. This rebellion blocks God's blessings from us. None of us is excluded from this problem of sin:

For all have sinned and fall short of the glory of God.

Romans 3:23

Some people feel that sin is an old-fashioned concept, but the Bible tells us that our sin separates us from God's blessings.

Surely the arm of the Lord is not too short to save, nor His ear too dull to hear. But your iniquities have separated you from your God; your sins have hidden His face from you, so that He will not hear.

Isaiah 59:1,2

Our good works and noble intentions are not sufficient to reinstate us to a standing where the holy God can bless us:

All of us have become like one who is unclean, and all our righteous acts are like filthy rags; we all shrivel up like a leaf, and like the wind our sins sweep us away.

Isaiah 64:6

God's plan of salvation is the provision of His love for a race of fallen, stubborn beings. Because the Almighty is holy, His standards are essential and can't be ignored. But, because *"God is love,"* He designed a way to reinstate those individuals who, out of sincere love for Him, would obey His instructions.

GOD'S SOLUTION

God's Spirit overshadowed a virgin named Mary, and the child that was conceived was therefore both God and man. God entered our world in human form as the son of Mary and the Son of God – Jesus, the Christ (or "Anointed One").

Jesus led a sinless life by complete obedience to Father God. Then, as our substitute, He took our place and our punishment.

Whereas the punishment for sin was death, and because He was just, God couldn't ignore sin, but He revealed in the Old Testament that He would receive a substitute payment for man's sins.

Animal sacrifices pointed to the day when God, in human form, would come to earth and be our substitute sacrifice – the Lamb of God. What God's holiness demanded, God's love provided.

For God so loved the world that He gave His one and only Son, that whoever believes in Him shall not perish but have eternal life.

John 3:16

Because Jesus was a perfect man, He could pay for our sins; because He was Eternal God, His blood paid for **all** who would come to Him.

Jesus willingly went to the cross and died as our sin substitute. He arose from the dead to demonstrate that God's holiness was satisfied. By rising from the dead, Jesus broke sin's power over us.

...He entered the Most Holy Place once for all by His own blood, having obtained eternal redemption... How much more, then, will the blood of Christ, Who through the eternal Spirit offered Himself unblemished to God, cleanse our consciences from acts that lead to death, so that we may serve the living God!

Hebrews 9:12b,14

This salvation is all of God. Going to church, doing good works, etc., will not save us. It is very hard for independent individuals to accept that they can do nothing to merit salvation.

For it is by grace you have been saved, through faith—and this is not from yourselves, it is the gift of God – not by works, so that no one can boast.

Ephesians 2:8,9

OUR RESPONSE

A free gift cannot be earned, but it must be accepted. An essential aspect of God's plan of salvation is that it separates between those who couldn't care less about God's will and those who, when they see the error of their ways, will repent, or turn from doing their own thing.

...unless you repent, you too will all perish.

Luke 13:3

I have declared to both Jews and Greeks that they must turn to God in repentance and have faith in our Lord Jesus.

Acts 20:21

We receive Jesus' payment for our sin by submitting to His Lordship over our life. Submission and obedience puts us back on the original path God designed for us.

That if you confess with your mouth, "Jesus is Lord," and believe in your heart God raised Him from the dead, you will be saved.

Romans 10:9

Do you want to receive God's gift of salvation right now?

Do you believe that Jesus Christ died on the cross for your sins? That He arose from the grave on the third day?

Will you turn from being the boss of your life and surrender to Jesus, and ask Him to be your Lord?

Here is a sample prayer. Ponder it, then put it in your own words and say it to God, if you truly mean it.

Dear Heavenly Father, I come to You admitting that I have sinned and have not done Your will. I believe that, out of love, you sent Jesus, Your Son, to die for my sin. I believe that He rose from the dead and has destroyed sin's power over my life. I turn from my sin and receive Jesus as my Savior and my Lord.

The exact wording is not as important as the heart response. Did you turn from being the lord of your own life and, in receiving Jesus, are you making Him your Lord?

This may seem like a simple prayer, yet it is a legal transaction, a covenant. If you were sincere, God will honor His Word and will save you and send His Holy Spirit to live inside you.

GROWING AS A CHRISTIAN

1. Read the Bible every day. Get an easy to understand translation, such as The New International Version (this is the translation used for Appendix A), The New Living Bible, or The New American Standard Bible (the translation used for most of this study).

Start reading at least a chapter a day. Begin with Matthew's gospel and read through the New Testament first; then begin reading in the Old Testament.

Make notes as you read, and write down any questions you may have to ask a Bible teacher later. Begin each Bible study with prayer for God's guidance.

Look up these verses on the importance of Bible study: 1 Peter 2:2; 2 Timothy 3:16, 17; Psalm 119:11; Psalm 1:1-3. Check the index of your Bible for the location of the books of the Bible.

2. Talk to God your Father in prayer, every day. Begin your prayer time like Jesus' example, with praise (Matthew 6:9). Confess any sin. 1 John 1:9 tells us the Lord will forgive us. Look up these verses to see what happens when we don't confess our sin: Psalm 66:18; Psalm 32:1-7.

Pray for others (Ephesians 6:18, 19; Colossians 4:2-4). Instead of worrying, pray (Philippians 4:6-7). Give thanks in your prayers (1 Thessalonians 5:16-18). Bring your requests to the Father in Jesus' name (John 16:23,24).

3. Beware of a new pull. Our enemy, Satan, wants to pull you down, discourage you and make you give up. Jesus said the first thing that would happen to us after we receive the Word would be that Satan would come to try to steal the seed ("I didn't feel anything; nothing happened"). Also, persecution, worry, cares of this world, and the love of sin will attempt to choke the word (Mark 4:3-20).

Resist the devil in the name of Jesus the very instant you recognize his temptation traps of sin and doubt: 1 Peter 5:6-9; James 4:6-8; Ephesians 6:10-18; 2 Corinthians 10:3-5.

When temptations or pressures increase, get together with another believer. The Lord wants us to strengthen each other (Galatians 6:1,2). We're to help others. This entire book is about winning the war against our enemy, Satan. **Learn all you can; share all you learn.**

4. Meet regularly with other Christians (Hebrews 10:24,25). Find a good church home where the Bible is taught, God is praised, Jesus is served, and the Holy Spirit is honored.

5. Look into being baptized in water (Matthew 28:19,20; Acts 10:47,48).

6. Begin seeking the baptism of the Holy Spirit. This is when Jesus pours out the power of the Holy Spirit on us. Study these verses: Luke 11:9-13; John 7:37-39; Acts 1:4-8; Acts 2:1-4; Acts 10:44-46. Chapters Nine and Ten in this book deal with this in more detail.

7. Begin sharing the story of God's love and salvation with others. You may be the only "preacher" some people will listen to (Romans 10:9-15).

For whoever will call upon the name of the Lord will be saved.

Romans 10:13

Appendix B

ARE DEMONS REALLY A PROBLEM?

We need to be careful saying something that the Bible doesn't clearly specify. A common question today is, "Can a Christian have a demon?" To answer such a query with a quick, flippant answer would require two or three clear Scriptures that say, "Yes, a believer can have a demon," or "No, a Christian can't be possessed or have a demon.

Many ministries today claim to cast demons out of believers. What they describe and what may actually be the case may be two different things. For instance, let's say that Clyde is prayed over because he has a terrible temper, and something leaves him. Before, he would strike his wife in fits of rage. Now he has a semblance of control. What took place? Did a demon "have Clyde" or was Clyde giving in to the demon's input without resisting?

If I understand "demon possession," you would have to say Clyde could not   keep from hitting his wife if he was angered. The demon that possessed him would make him hit his wife if he wanted to or not. One easy way to test Clyde to see if he was powerless would be to get Clyde very angry at his wife, but quickly bring a huge policeman into the room (ugly and mean would help). If a demon was possessing Clyde so that he couldn't help hitting his wife, my theory is that the presence of a law enforcement officer would not restrain the demon and Clyde would go ahead and hit his wife in the presence of the policeman. If he did, I would say he was possessed.

Can a Christian have a demon? Who wants one? Browse over the following verses and draw your own conclusions.

1. Mat 10:1-8 - Jesus had His disciples preach first, then cast out demons, perhaps to make the people believers and thereby give the right for deliverance [otherwise the people belonged to Satan - Eph 2:1-3]

2. Mat 12:44 - Jesus said that demons can go into houses that are *"swept and put in order"*

3. *Mat 13:24,25 - in a Kingdom of God parable, Jesus said "while men were sleeping, his enemy came and sowed tares..."*

4. Mat 15:22-28 - the Canaanite woman's daughter:

   a. The girl was *"cruelly possessed"* - v. 22

   b. Jesus said that deliverance was the *"Children's Bread"*

   c. Deliverance is called healing - v. 28

   Why would deliverance be called "Children's Bread" if it wasn't for God's kids? And why would it be for God's kids if they couldn't have a demon?

5. Mat 16:23 - Jesus called Peter *"Satan"*

6. John 13:27 - Satan entered Judas, one of the chosen 12

7. Mark 16:15-18 - Jesus' commission to the church was:

   a. Go and preach - and thereby make Christians

   b. Baptize them in water

   c. And then follow this by casting out the demons: *And these signs will* **follow** *those who believe: In My name they will cast out demons; they will speak with new tongues; 16:17 (nkj)*

8. Act 5:3 - Satan *"filled"* Ananias' heart, a member of the congregation, (4:32)

9. Acts 5:14 - it appears that of the multitude added to the number of believers, some were delivered of demons (v.16)

10. Acts 8:4 - Philip preached Christ in Samaria and later in verse 7 we're told that unclean spirits came out of people

11. Acts 8:12,13 - Simon the magician believed and was baptized in Jesus' name, but when he tried to buy the power to give the Holy Spirit, Peter said, *"You are in the bondage of iniquity"* - v. 23

12. Acts 19:12 - Paul preached in Ephesus for some time and deliverance took place afterwards

13. Acts 20:30 - sounds like some Christians will go off the deep end: Also from among yourselves men will rise up, speaking perverse things, to draw away the disciples after them¬selves.

14. Rom 7:21 - did Paul have a problem?   I find then the principle that evil is present in me, the one who wishes to do good.   Rom 7:21

   a. In the verse before this he denies responsibility for the problem: *But if I am doing the very thing I do not wish, I am no longer the one doing it, but sin which dwells in me.   Rom 7:20*

   b. Which sounds a lot like God's warning to Cain: ...*sin is crouching at the door; and its desire is for you, but you must master it."   Gen 4:7*

   c. In Rom 7:23 he says there's a war going on inside him: *but I see a different law in the members of my body, waging war against the law of my mind, and making me a prisoner of the law of sin which is in my members.* Rom 7:23

   d. Sounds like what some say: the body can have demons, but not the spirit

15. 1 Cor 3:1-4 - carnal Christians are fleshly and can get into jealousy and strife, which is called demonic wisdom later in James 3:14,15

16. 1 Cor 5:5 - the man caught in incest was turned over to "*Satan for the destruction of the flesh so his spirit could be saved*" – was he saved already?

17. 1 Cor 5:11 - so-called brothers can do idols and idols do demons: *No, but I say that the things which the Gentiles sacrifice, they sacrifice to*

*demons, and not to God; and I do not want you to become **sharers in demons**. 1 Cor 10:20*

18. 1 Cor 8:10 - if a weak brother sees you eating food sacrificed to idols, he can be **ruined.** How? Because the meat has demons (10:20) and they will overcome the weak person if he eats some. Probably via the guilt   (v.12)

19. 1 Cor 9:26 - Paul boxed, but not against the air (remember Rom 7:23). What was in the balance? *But I keep under my body, and bring it into subjection: lest that by any means, when I have preached to others, I myself should be a castaway.*   1 Cor 9:27 (KJV)   **Sounds serious!**

20. 1 Cor 12:7 - spiritual gifts were given to the Body for the *"common good"*, and if *"distinguishing of spirits"* (v.10) is for deliverance ministry, then believers need this gift to set them free

21. 2 Cor 1:9,10 - Paul was *"delivered"* from an *"inner sentence of death"* - and from v.8, we could say it was a spirit of depression

22. 2 Cor 2:10,11 - Paul pushed the believers to forgive so that *"no advantage be taken   of us by Satan"*

23. 2 Cor 6:14-16 - Paul warns against fellowshipping with idols (re: demons, 10:20)

24. 2 Cor 10:3-5 - Paul saw the war as an inner war against *"fortresses"*

25. 2 Cor 11:3,4 - Paul was *"afraid"* that believers could be led astray by *"**receiving** a different spirit"*

26. 2 Cor 11:14,15 - our job is made harder because Satan's servants disguise themselves as *"servants of righteousness"* and he poses as an *"angel of light"* – but their works give them away.

27. 2 Cor 12:7 - Paul had a *"messenger of Satan"* because of pride, and note that he didn't ask for healing, but that *"**it** would depart"* - v.8

28. 2 Cor 13:5 - he closes this book with a warning to *"test yourself"*

29. Gal 2:4 - the Galatians were warned of bondage

30. Gal 3:1 - some Galatians were *"bewitched"* - sounds like some kind of demonic control

31. Gal 4:9 - Paul feared some had become *"enslaved all over again"*

32. Gal 5:1 - believers can be *"subjected again to a yoke of slavery"* and thus *"fall from grace"* (v.4)

33. Eph 1:18-23 - if demons were of no problem to believers, why bother to tell us we have authority over them? And why tell us we get to tell them we have authority over them (Eph 3:10)?

34. We're to *"lay aside"* (NASB) or *"put off"* (KJV) the *"old self which is being* (present tense) *corrupted"* –   and if we don't (v. 27), we'll *"give the devil"* an opportunity

35. Eph 6:12 - our true enemy is not ourselves. Or others.

36. 1 Thes 2:18 - Paul wanted to visit Thessalonica, but more than once he was *"hindered by Satan,"* so don't feel bad... BE ON THE ALERT.

37. 1 Thes 3:5 - Paul *"feared"* the tempter might undo his labor

38. 1 Tim 1:20 - Hymenaeus & Alexander were *"delivered over to Satan"* because they were suffering from the *"shipwreck of their faith"* (v. 19)

39. 1 Tim 3:7 - elder candidates must have a good reputation so they don't fall into the *"snare of the devil"*

40. 1 Tim 4:1 - some will pay attention to demons and *"fall away."* If a believer can "fall away" from the faith, then, without controversy, they could be possessed by a spirit at that point. But, if a spirit could trick a believer into falling away, then we'd better stop arguing about believers having demons and make sure we're not giving them any open doors.

41. 1 Tim 5:14 - some had *"given the enemy an occasion for reproach"* and ended up turning *"aside to follow Satan"*- v. 15

42. 2 Tim 2:26 - some argumentative folks were *"held captive by Satan to do his will"*

43. Jam 3:6 - hell *"sets on fire the course of our life"*. If hell can do this to the course of our life, how much control can demons get?

44. Jam 3:14,15 - bitter jealousy and selfish ambition is *"demonic wisdom"*

45. Jam 4:7 - what happens if a believer doesn't *"resist the devil"*?

46. 1 Pet 4:7,8 - what if our faith is too weak to resist? [Verse 10 seems to blame all the suffering First Peter talks about, on the devil.]

47. 2 Pet 2:19 - *"For by what a man is overcome, by this he is enslaved"* is a warning to believers. *For if after they have escaped the defilements of the world by the knowledge of the Lord and Savior Jesus Christ, they are again entangled in them and are overcome, the last state has become worse for them than the first.*   2 Pet 2:20

48. 1 Jhn 4:1 - what happens if we *"believe every spirit"*? See Rom 6:16

49.   Rev 12:10,11 - what if some believers didn't resist the devil with the 3 weapons because they thought the "guilt" was just them? "My flesh."

50. Rev 16:13-15 - why on earth did the Lord put verse 15 in with 13 & 14? *And I saw coming out of the mouth of the dragon and out of the mouth of the beast and out of the mouth of the false prophet, three unclean spirits like frogs;(14) for they are spirits of demons, performing signs, which go out to the kings of the whole world, to gather them together for the war of the great day of God, the Almighty. (15) ("Behold, I am coming like a thief. Blessed is the one who stays awake and keeps his garments, lest he walk about naked and men see his shame.")*   Rev 16:13-15

Can a Christian have demon problems? Read carefully the words of our Lord Jesus from the New King James Version...

But let your "Yes" be "Yes," and your "No" be "No." For whatever is more than these is from **the evil one.**

Matthew 5:37 nkj

Our conversation may have more enemy input than we've realized.

May the love of Jesus Christ keep you in the center of His perfect will.

Yet in all these things we are more than conquerors through Him who loved us.   Romans 8:37

www.RoyalMountainMinistry.com

Other Material From RMM

PAMPHLETS

Just Relax

Changing Pictures

Victory Over Anger

Conquering Curses

Medicine that Heals

Victory Through Hard Times

The Place of Women in the Church

Blended Families & New Beginnings

Eternal Security or Security of the Faithful

BOOKS

The Doorway to the Abundant Life

SRD: The Traveler's Guide

The Law of Rest

Eyes of Faith

Loving God

The River